The Color of My Resilience:

A Guided Self-Care Journal for Black Women

USA TODAY BESTSELLING AUTHOR

N.D. JONES

Kuumba Publishing
1325 Bedford Avenue
#32374
Pikesville, MD
kuumbapublishing.com

Cover Design: Ravenborn Covers
Coloring Pages: Ekra Design

The Color of My Resilience: A Guided Self-Care Journal for Black Women/ N.D. Jones. -- 1st ed.
ISBN: 978-1-7352998-7-7

This Journal Belongs To:

CONTENTS

CONTENTS

Introduction

My Why and What

Strong Black Woman. Black Girl Magic. Tropes or truths? Affirmations or Motivations? All of the above or none at all? As a Black woman and author of fantasy novels with magic-wielding witches, I must admit that I love the concept of Black females as magic users. Indeed, all my heroines are, in varying respects, strong Black women. However, they are not strong Black women because they can manipulate elemental energy, heal diseases with a thought, or even transform into a fire-breathing dragon but because they are, at their core, women with wants, desires, and flaws.

They are beautifully, wonderfully imperfect. They struggle, and they fall. They love, and they hate. They have a heroine's arc in which they overcome an enemy—internal, external, or both. They utilize magic as they progress through their heroine's journey because they are fantasy characters with extraordinary powers readers want to see them use to the greatest effect. But magic takes them only so far. The use of magic is not the key to solving their issues—the conflict on which their arc hinges. The best conflicts for a heroine are the ones that cannot be pummeled into submission or magicked out of existence. Conflicts of the mind and heart are what keeps a reader riveted to the story, turning pages or swiping left. Readers want to cheer for a worthy heroine. And what heroine is more deserving of the title of Black Girl Magic than one who bleeds yet digs deep in search of resilience? One who cries, curses, and sometimes despairs but manages to find the roots of the nearest tree of life and pull herself up—wobbly knees and shaky hands but steady feet.

Imperfect. Flawed. Resilient.

Strong Black Woman. These three words can motivate, but they can also intimidate and misrepresent. They have been used as both an insult and as a rallying cry—an acknowledgment of our intersectionality of oppression and minimization of our struggles and pain.

There is no otherworldly magic in a Black woman's capacity to survive, no more than there is in her ability to thrive despite racism, sexism, classism, homophobia, and so on. At the end of a tiring day, Black Girl Magic is old-fashioned grit and perseverance. It is tears, laughter, and faith—love, exhaustion, and frustration. Black Girl Magic is a wily cat to some. A unicorn of myth for others. But to those who can wrangle it into submission, it is hope found at the bottom of a jar of quarters.

Use in case of an emergency.

Strong Black Woman. Black Girl Magic. Who are we? Who do we want to become? My journey has brought me to this place, not a concealed stop Harriet would've made on her dangerous trek from the south to the north but a woman's mission of freedom and self-actualization. In what world—fantasy or real—must a woman undertake her heroine's journey alone? None. Let us build our resilience together.

Not-So-Fun Facts

- 44.3% of Black women die of heart disease and cancer

- 14.9% of Black women age 1-19 years die from homicide

- 5.5% of Black women age 1-19 die from suicide

- 6.7% of Black women age 20-44 die from homicide

- 29.8% of Black women age 45-64 die of cancer

- 25.3% of Black women age 65-84 die of cancer

- 27.2% of Black women age 85 years and older die of heart disease

BLACK LIVES MATTER

Source: Centers for Disease Control and Prevention, *Leading Causes of Death - Females - Non-Hispanic black - United States, 2017* (2019)

How This Book is Organized

The book is divided into five chapters and three parts. The first chapter—The Woman with Resolve: How Do I Persevere?—provides an opportunity for you to describe your struggles and to reflect on your resilience. The other four chapters—The Woman in the Mirror, The Woman with Heart, The Woman with Helping Hands, and the Woman of Good Health—cover aspects of resilience, such as self-care and management of emotions. This is the guidebook portion of the book. Each chapter includes topics that contribute to the Not-So-Fun Facts listed above. Keep this question in mind: What is within my sphere of control and influence? Your answers are the rich soil from which the most flagrant perennials will grow. You are your best change agent.

The second part of the book is the journal. While there are opportunities to journal in part one, part two provides six different reflection strategies—long and short reflections, notes of appreciation, artful thinking, letters to emotions, and perspective writing from a selection of timely and relevant topics. You may find you prefer one or two methods over the others. Comfort level and engagement are essential, but consider trying them all once. Sometimes, a gem is hidden in plain sight.

The third part of the book—Leveling Up—contains copies of the forms and reflection pages from part one. Think of this book as a "living" document. The topics and activities are not timebound. They are meant to serve you for years to come—long after you have filled the pages with your wisdom, happiness, and, yes, even with your heartache. When you brainstorm a Month of Joy activities in part one, for example, turn the task into a healthy, lifelong practice. When you identify your allies at home, work and school, allow the importance of forming allies to follow you through every aspect of your life. Section three is a reminder that resilience is as much about knowing, doing, and reflecting as it is about knowing, doing, and reflecting over and again.

Finally, there are poems and essays written by Black women. From a college student to a small business owner to a USA Today bestselling author, these women have opened their hearts and shared their stories of resilience.

What This Book Is and What It Is Not

The Color of My Resilience is a guided journal intended to foster and support self-awareness and reflection in a safe environment. Despite the personal and sensitive nature of the topics herein, this book does not offer advice or seek to replace medical treatment. If you are in therapy or counseling, follow orders from your medical professional. If you require medical support, seek the necessary assistance from a qualified and licensed professional.

Finally, all journeys do not need to be undertaken alone or in secret. Indeed, some of the best trips are those traveled with others. Two key ingredients to building resilience are the willingness to experience vulnerability and the strength to say no.

On behalf of those who love and care about you, thank you for choosing to increase your resilience.

Be safe.
Be strong.
Be healthy.

PART 1
GUIDEBOOK

"WHEN I FOUND I HAD CROSSED THAT LINE, I LOOKED AT MY HANDS TO SEE IF I WAS THE SAME PERSON. THERE WAS SUCH A GLORY OVER EVERYTHING."

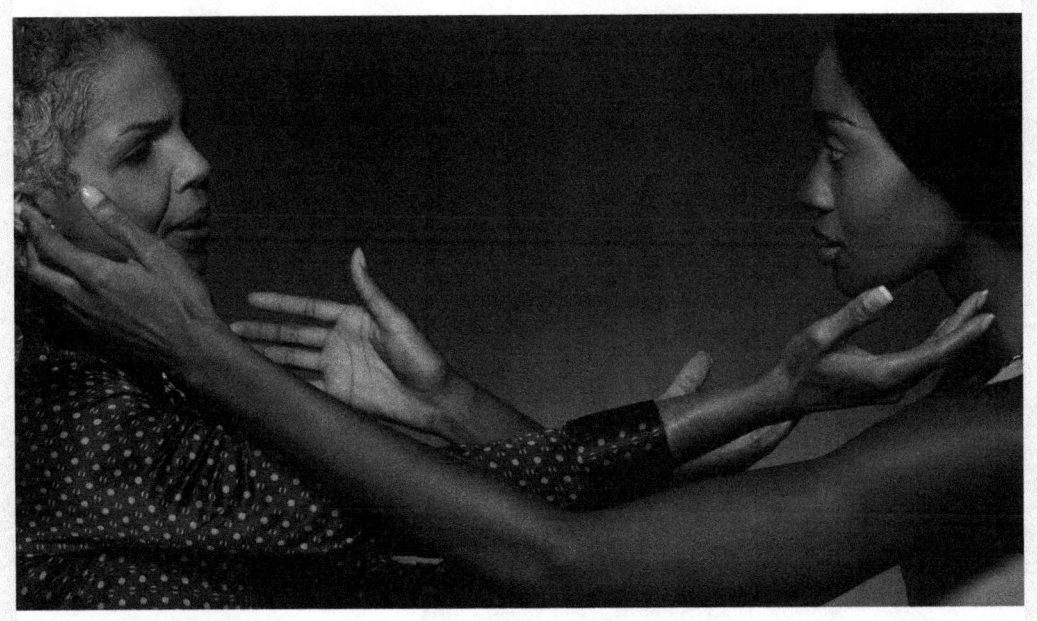

Harriet Tubman

The Woman with Resolve

How Do I Persevere?

What it means for me to be a Black woman in the 21st century

_____

_____

_____

_____

_____

_____

_____

_____

_____

_____

_____

_____

_____

_____

_____

_____

_____

_____

_____

_____

_____

_____

_____

_____

_____

_____

_____

MIDNIGHT MUSINGS

NKOSAZANA KEMRAHA
Student, Towson University

As I breathe in the midnight air
Basking in the
Cool salty spray of water.
Ever far away on the waves, and
foamy water rushes on the beach.
Gentle yet dangerous, the deep blue.
Here to sweep me up and fold me
Inside it's depth gently,
Just enough for me to feel weightless.
Knots of nerves leave me as I
Lean back and embrace my
Mortality fully, no bullshit.
No one to pretend for,
Over and under the waves move around me.
Pushing and pulling reminding me that within the
Quiet there is noise; and stillness hides chaos.
Remember to be cautious of those who remain
Silent but aware. whether you take heed of it or not
Think of all the times and circumstances of the past
Unfinished and saved for last.
Vague instances that are lost to time.

WHAT'S MY WHY?

_____

_____

_____

_____

_____

_____

_____

_____

_____

_____

_____

_____

_____

_____

_____

_____

_____

Graphics used with permission from Akiim DeShay, Owner of BlackDemographics.com

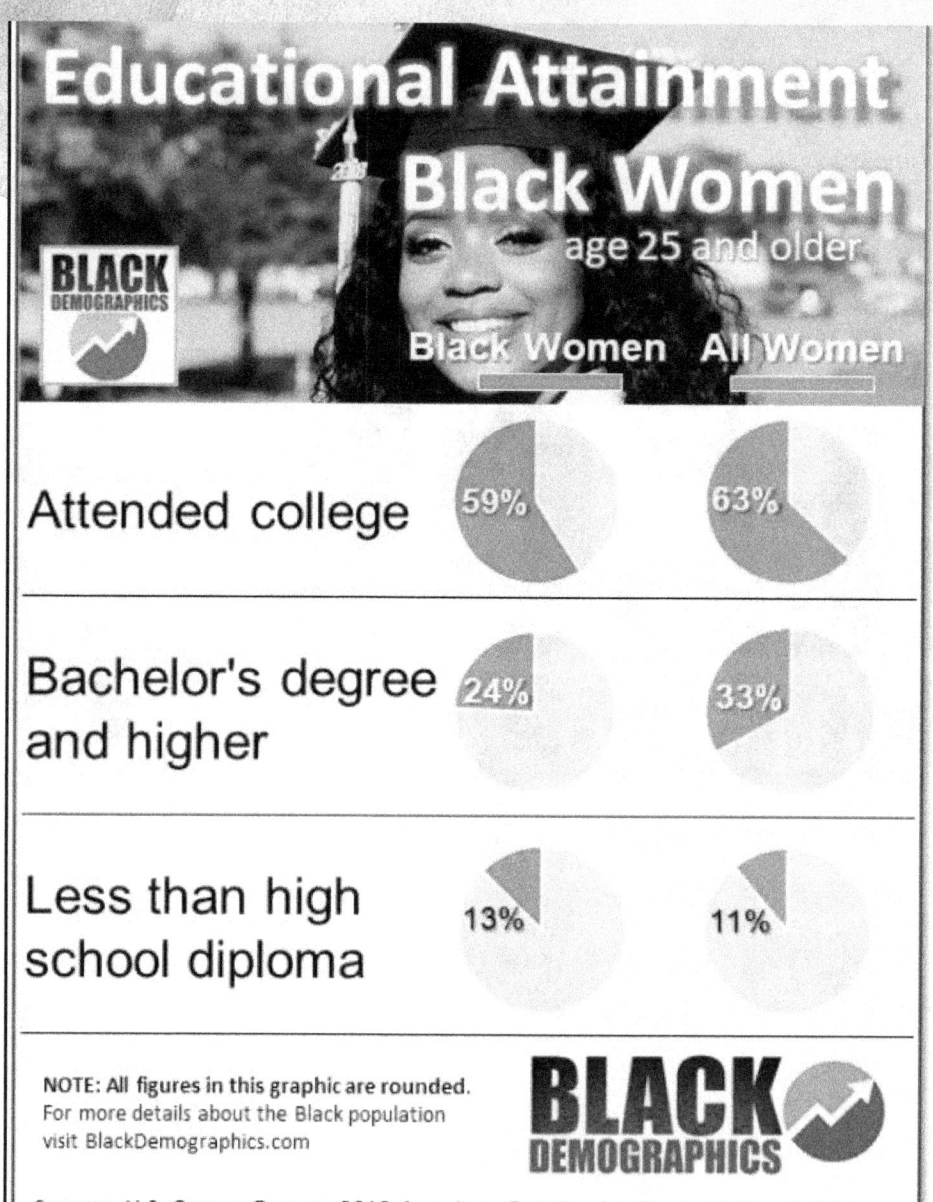

Educational Attainment
Black Women
age 25 and older

Black Women   All Women

Attended college   59%   63%

Bachelor's degree and higher   24%   33%

Less than high school diploma   13%   11%

NOTE: All figures in this graphic are rounded. For more details about the Black population visit BlackDemographics.com

BLACK DEMOGRAPHICS

Source: U.S. Census Bureau, 2018 American Community Survey 1-Year Estimates
Created by BlackDemographics.com

Occupation Type
Black Women
age 16 and older

Black women   All women

White collar

For the purpose of this chart white collar occupations include but are not limited to jobs in management, business, computers, office, legal, education, etc.

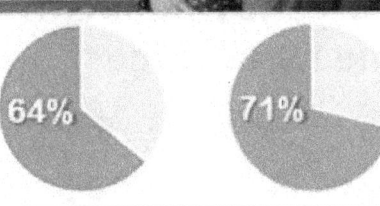

64%   71%

Blue collar

Blue collar occupations include employment in construction, maintenance and repair, installation, production, transportation, etc.

8%   8%

Service occupations

Service occupations include healthcare support, protective service, food preparation and serving, etc.

28%   21%

NOTE: All figures in this graphic are rounded. For more details about the Black population visit BlackDemographics.com

Source: U.S. Census Bureau, 2018 American Community Survey 1-Year Estimates
Created by **BlackDemographics.com**

Black Women
Households & Responsibilities

Black women   **All women**

Household Headed by Woman*

27%   12%

Gave Birth While Married

37%   66%

Live Below Poverty Level

24%   14%

NOTE: All figures in this graphic are rounded. For more details about the Black population visit BlackDemographics.com

BLACK DEMOGRAPHICS

Source: U.S. Census Bureau, 2018 American Community Survey 1-Year Estimates, *2017 American Community Survey 1-Year Estimates
Created by BlackDemographics.com

Relationships Black Women

age 15 and older

BLACK DEMOGRAPHICS

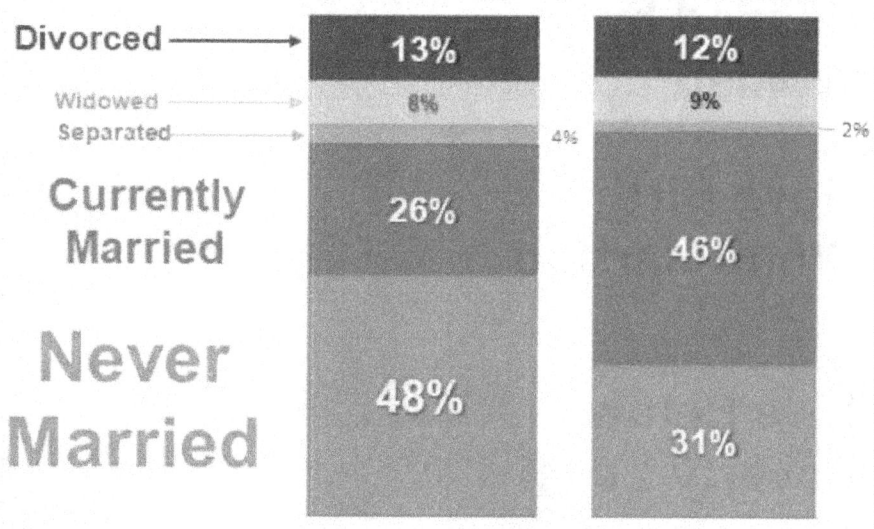

	Black Women	All Women
Divorced	13%	12%
Widowed	8%	9%
Separated	4%	2%
Currently Married	26%	46%
Never Married	48%	31%

NOTE: All figures in this graphic are rounded. For more details about the Black population visit BlackDemographics.com

BLACK DEMOGRAPHICS

Source: U.S. Census Bureau, 2018 American Community Survey 1-Year Estimates
Created by BlackDemographics.com

20

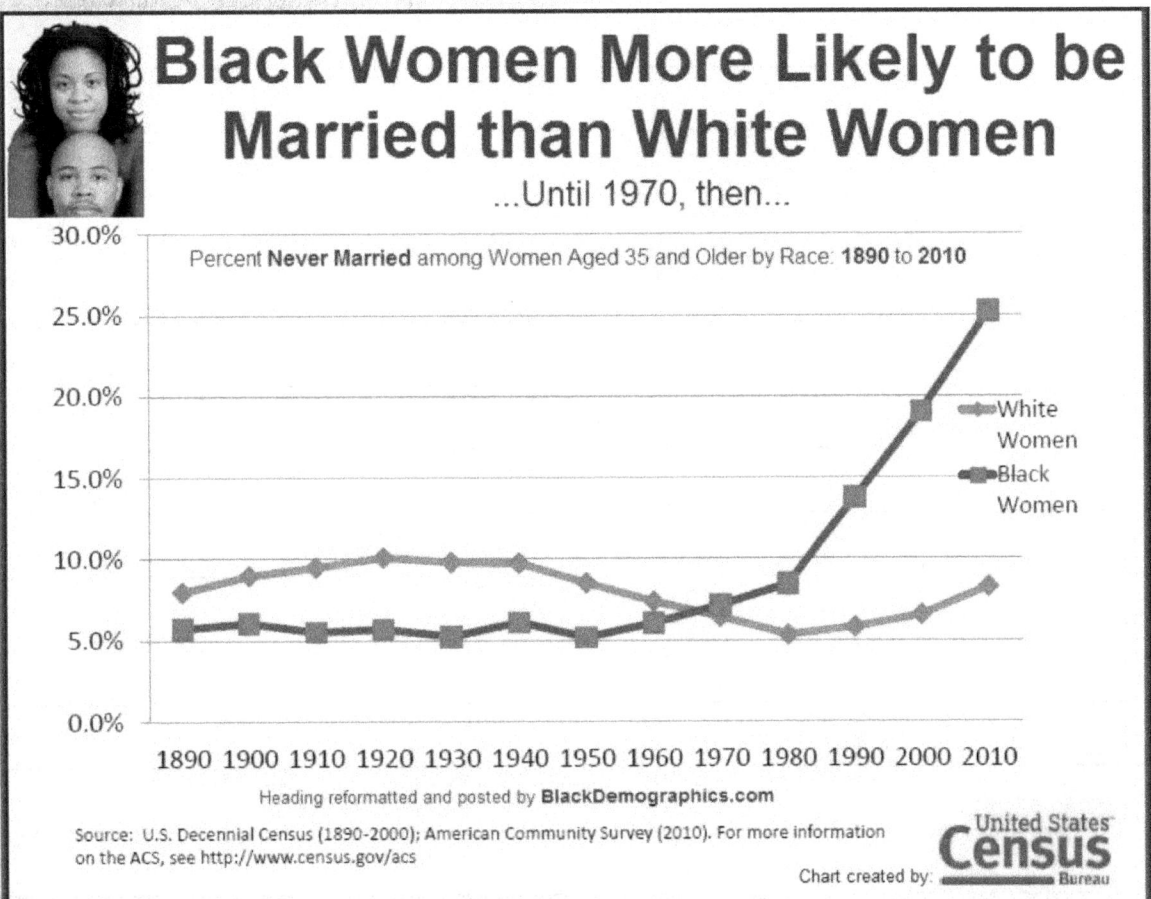

Black Women More Likely to be Married than White Women

...Until 1970, then...

Percent **Never Married** among Women Aged 35 and Older by Race: **1890** to **2010**

White Women

Black Women

Heading reformatted and posted by **BlackDemographics.com**

Source: U.S. Decennial Census (1890-2000); American Community Survey (2010). For more information on the ACS, see http://www.census.gov/acs

Chart created by: United States Census Bureau

21

WHAT'S ON MY MIND?

_____

_____

_____

_____

_____

_____

_____

_____

_____

_____

_____

_____

_____

*"Never be afraid to sit awhile
and think."*

LORRAINE
HANSBERRY

RESILIENCE

What words, images, and people come
to mind when you think of the
word *resilience?*

RESILIENCE

What words, images, and people come to mind when you think of the word *resilience*?

RESILIENCE

Psychology Today in Positive Psychology

"Resilience is that ineffable quality that allows some people to be knocked down by life and come back stronger than ever. Rather than letting failure overcome them and drain their resolve, they find a way to rise from the ashes."

Merriam Webster

"An ability to recover from or adjust easily to misfortune or change."

American Psychological Association

Process of adapting well in the face of diversity, trauma, tragedy, threats, or significant sources of stress--such as family and relationship problems, serious health problems, or workplace and financial stressors.".

WHAT'S ON MY MIND?

_____

_____

_____

_____

_____

_____

_____

_____

_____

_____

_____

_____

_____

_____

"Never be afraid to sit awhile and think."

LORRAINE HANSBERRY

THE STRUGGLE IS REAL

Reflect on a time in your life when you weren't as resilient as you
wanted or needed to be.

What were the consequences?
What were the barriers to your resilience?
What lesson(s) did you learn?

THE STRUGGLE IS REAL

_____

_____

_____

_____

_____

_____

_____

_____

_____

_____

_____

_____

_____

"Binge drinking, smoking (cigarettes and marijuana), illicit drug use and prescription pain reliever misuse are more frequent among Black and African American adults with mental illnesses."

"Black and African American people living below poverty are twice as likely to report serious psychological distress than those living over 2x the poverty level."

Mental Health

"Serious mental illness (SMI) rose among all ages of Black and African American people between 2008 and 2018."

"Adult Blacks and African Americans are more likely to have feelings of sadness, hopelessness, and worthlessness than adult whites."

Source: Mental Health America (2020) *Black and African American Communities and Mental Health*

"African American females, grades 9-12, were 70 percent more likely to attempt suicide in 2017, as compared to non-Hispanic white females of the same age."

Source: U.S. Department of Health and Human Services Office of Minority Health (2019), *Mental and Behavioral Health - African Americans*

My Mental Health

My Mental Health

_____
_____
_____
_____
_____
_____
_____
_____
_____
_____
_____
_____
_____
_____
_____
_____

My Mental Health

WHAT'S ON MY MIND?

_____

_____

_____

_____

_____

_____

_____

_____

_____

_____

_____

_____

_____

_____

*"Never be afraid to sit awhile
and think."*
LORRAINE
HANSBERRY

bell hooks

"If we give our children sound self-love, they will be able to deal with whatever life puts before them."

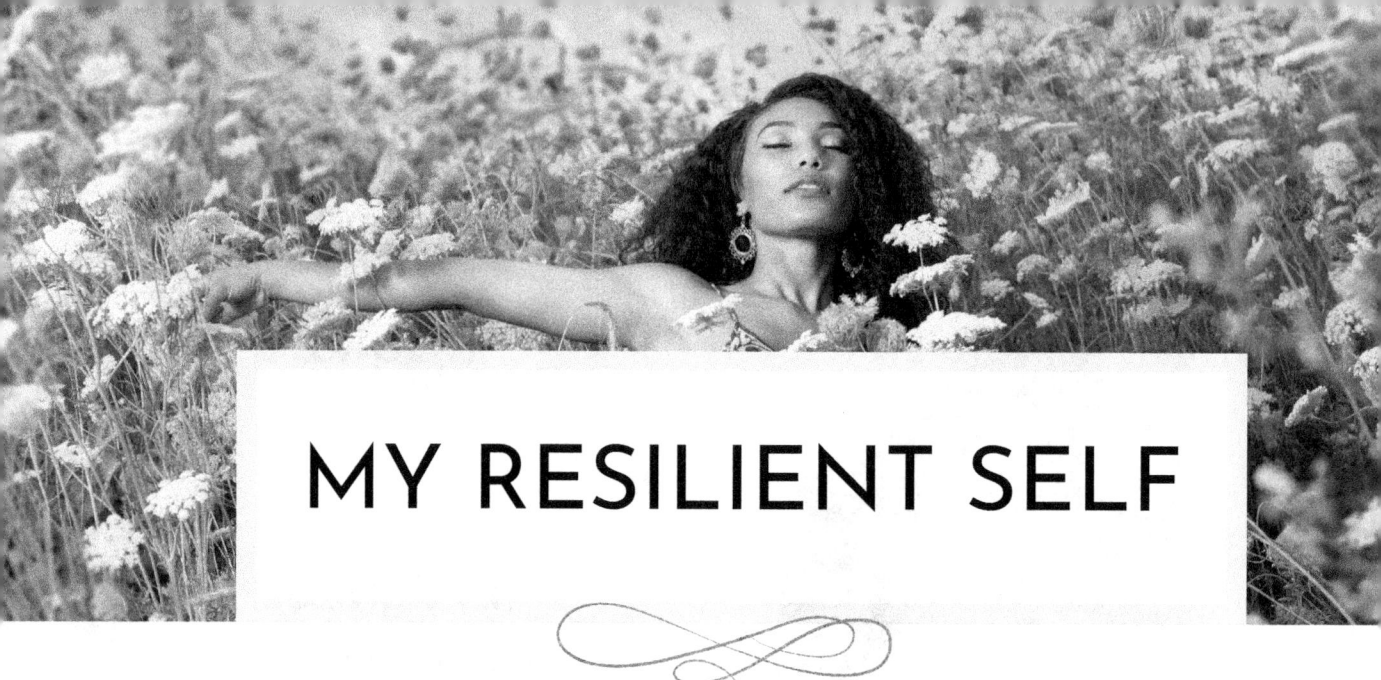

MY RESILIENT SELF

Reflect on a time in your life when you felt truly resilient.

What happened?
What supports were available to you?
What lesson(s) did you learn?

_____

_____

_____

_____

_____

_____

_____

_____

_____

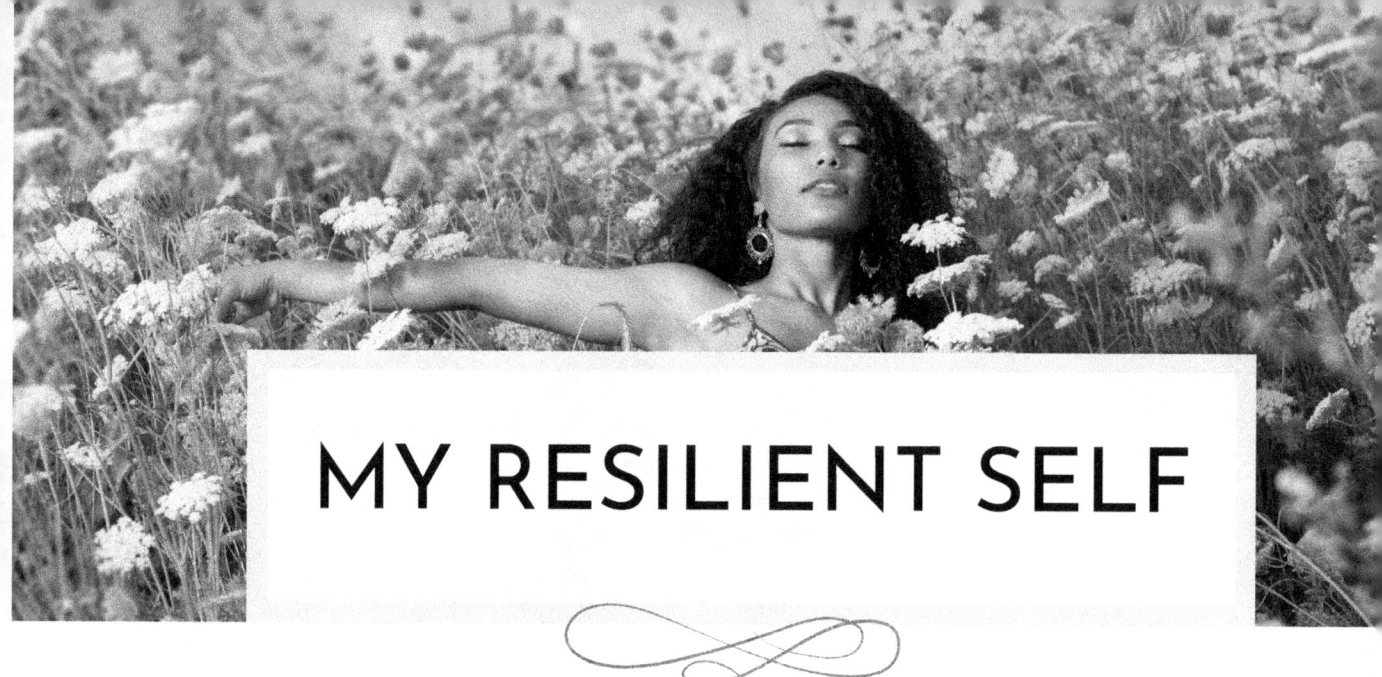

MY RESILIENT SELF

Reflect on a time in your life when you felt truly resilient.

What happened?
What supports were available to you?
What lesson(s) did you learn?

_____

_____

_____

_____

_____

_____

_____

_____

WHAT'S ON MY MIND?

_____

_____

_____

_____

_____

_____

_____

_____

_____

_____

_____

_____

_____

_____

_____

*"Never be afraid to sit awhile
and think."*

LORRAINE
HANSBERRY

LEARNING TO CRY

DARIEL RAYE
USA Today Bestselling Author

Falling into the car seat after an especially long day at the mental health center— longer because my body did not feel like my own, I prayed just like I did every day, placing my clients' problems in God's hands as I left to face my own. Swollen ankles and occasional dizziness meant I needed to make time in my hectic schedule for a visit to the doctor, so I did. My doctor scheduled a battery of tests, and that day, it was time to receive the results.

"Are you sitting down?"

I sat on the side of the bed. The nurse always called with messages and test results, but today, it was the doctor. Sickness was no stranger to me. Born with a heart murmur, the portent of health problems had been constant as far back as I could remember. Rheumatic heart at age five led to a prescription of daily antibiotics to protect me from infections because a common cold could kill me. Subsequent debilitating rheumatoid arthritis at age fifteen and myriad health problems along the way brutally equipped me for the battle I faced. Still, despite the unwanted preparation, it's not easy to accept that your life will never be the same.

The room faded as I ended the call with my doctor and called my mother. Who you call in times of crisis is revelatory. I quickly relayed the news. "Mama, I'm on my way to the hospital. The doctor wants me to see a specialist because he thinks I have kidney failure."

Over the next few months, life as I knew it came to an abrupt halt. I underwent painful procedures and several surgeries in thirty days. Both of my kidneys were failing due to complications from the rheumatoid disorder from childhood, and over the course of that year, I underwent more surgeries than I could count on both hands. There was no time to acknowledge what was happening, let alone adjust. The tears I cried during that call to my mother were the last physical signs of grief I showed for a long time.

Despite being a daddy's girl, I had no tears for his funeral - the man who kept track of every family member's keys, my on-call mechanic, even when I was married, the guardian who drove across town and let himself into my house at 6:30 am to check on me after my divorce because he was "in the neighborhood." In the mid-stages of Alzheimer's disease, when I started dialysis, we lost him after watching his brilliant mind fracture and fade. Numbness consumed me.

 Survival required all of my energy as anger and depression hi-jacked my positive outlook and turned me into someone I'd never met. I had been "good," it wasn't fair, and I had to deal with this new reality for the rest of my life. I felt God nudging me onto the path I'd minimized.
 There's always something, an interest, a gift, an ability, or even a belief that pulls us back, centers, and grounds us when we lose our way. I've often heard people say you should never question God, but who understands better when we vent or seek to understand? So, I vented, finally learning lessons that eventually gave me peace.

Slowly, amid my ranting, the anger began to subside in stages as I incorporated new rituals and ways of thinking into my 'Type A' perspective. Just as I'd always given my clients' problems to God at the end of the day, I learned to do the same with my own, opening my conversation with God each morning. Instead of checking my calendar and rushing through my 'to-do' list for the day, I meditated and prayed, focusing on the many good things in my life instead of lamenting the losses.

Some drifted away for reasons related to their own lack instead of my own, but their disappearance helped me appreciate my loved ones who supported me even more. I have always been extremely independent, and learning to depend on others is still a work in progress.

My life has changed drastically since the kidney failure diagnosis, June 2005, requiring a new vision and granting a second chance to get things right. I value quality relationships, appreciate the creative gifts God has given, laugh, cry, and live with less 'busy-ness' and more joy – singing, playing instruments, creating art, and writing.

ZORA NEALE HURSTON

"Sometimes, I feel discriminated against, but it does not make me angry. It merely astonishes me. How can any deny themselves the pleasure of my company? It's beyond me."

TYPES OF ABUSE

CULTURAL IDENTITY

PHYSICAL

ECONOMIC/FINANCIAL

SEXUAL

MENTAL/PSYCHOLOGICAL

VERBAL/EMOTIONAL

RESILIENCE

Cultural Identity

A person's cultural identity is used to harm them (Ex: use of racial slurs; denial of religious practices; use of homophobic language; anti-dreadlock or braids policy)

Physical

Harm to a person's body or a threat of harm (Ex: hitting; kickin; strangling; reckless driving)

Economic/Financial

An exertion of power and control via financial means (Ex: creation of debt; denial of access to bank account; prevention of employment)

Sexual

Forced sexual acts and/or using sex as a weapon (Ex: rape; criticism of sexual performance; restriction of access to birth control and condoms)

Mental/Psychological

Words and actions that serve to diminish a person's sense of self and mental sanity (Ex: repeat accusation of being "crazy"; denial of factual events; lectures; digital spying)

Verbal/Emotional

Words used that can damage a person's sense of self and self-esteem (Ex: name-calling; derogatory "pet names"; public embarrassment)

Source: Reach Beyond Domestic Violence (2017)

THE SHE, SHE WANTS TO BE (MORGAN LEE)

NAKEISHA SAVAGE, Ed.D.
Education Leader

Let me get this straight
So you
wanted me
To believe
That she
Couldn't be
The she
She wanted to be

You wanted me
To force her
You wanted to coerce her
To fit into your definition
Your expectation
Your discrimination
Neglect her personal equation
And submit to your summation

You telling me young women can only be celebrated
Only allowed to be graduated
If they are silenced
Sis, you wildin'

NAKEISHA SAVAGE, Ed.D.
Education Leader

You're seated in a whole contradiction
Of your diversity policy
Words that praise individuality
Just blatant hypocrisy
Based in your own convictions
Your preferred depiction
Of what a woman should look like

Don't know what you thought
But this teen has been taught
That she got a voice
And she got choice

And what you not gonna do
Boo Boo
Is to convince her
Or try to dismiss her
Or try to unlist her

Did you really try to suspend her
For things she didn't do
False claims no truth
No proof

How could you really think that you
Could bully my daughter
One thing that I taught her
Is mommy got your back see
Come for her, you come for me

NAKEISHA SAVAGE, Ed.D.
Education Leader

Keep playing and imma let all this Savage free
Foot to that neck
Best you not forget
I am her biggest advocate
And you will respect her
Cause this one, right here
She's mine

Fully equipped with a whole tribe
All ride or dies
She was born to shine
My one and only child

So she ain't wearing no dress
No skirt, no gown
Draped to the ground
She gonna wear this suit
Dressed in her truth
That you will not dictate
Keep your homophobic hate

It spills from you
It limits you

My sista
My sista

NAKEISHA SAVAGE, Ed.D.
Education Leader

We are all black women, sis
What happened to empowerment
Being your sista's strength
Pouring into our black children
Supporting and uplifting them

But you not lifting them
You trying to cripple them
Your mind is trippin' and
You won't dim her light

Because she shines bright
In her own excellence
Black, gifted and talented

I'm not just saying this
Because I'm her mother
I am and have been the mother
Of so many others

As educators, it is our responsibility
To love them
Accept them

Mirrored reflections
Of strength
Resilience
Determination

NAKEISHA SAVAGE, Ed.D.
Education Leader

Intimidation
Is what you won't do
I promise you

She is life
She is fire
She is love
She is art
She is my heart

She is
Who she is
And who she wants to be

And neither you or me
Have the audacity
To try to transform her
Get her to conform to
Anything other than
The black, beautiful woman
She is and is destined to be

Authentically
Unapologetically
My Morgan Lee

HEART'S CANVAS

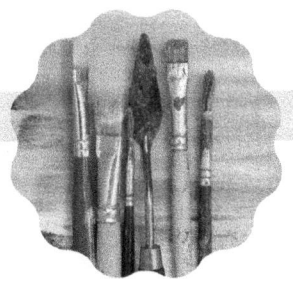

POWERFUL

AHYOKA YAMINA (LATISHA PRICE)
Lecturer, Morgan State University

Discovering who I am has been the general theme of my life's story. As women, we tend to struggle with relationships because of our deep loving and caring nature. We love so deeply that we forget to love ourselves in the process. The one lesson in life that I had to learn was to embrace the woman I have grown to be and to accept the role I play in this world. My childhood was fair, but I experienced some traumas that I never really dealt with as an adult. These traumas led me to tolerate physical, emotional, and mental abuse from men. I didn't understand what I experienced then was affecting me as an adult. Truth be told, I am still working on healing myself to this day, but it is different now because I have overcome so much, and now I know who I am. I spent most of my adult years making bad decisions and attached to unhealthy relationships. I guess you are wondering what those traumas were? Unfortunately, I must save that story for my autobiography. I can tell you that I've subconsciously been hiding who I am from the world because I've been afraid of rejection and abandonment.

The year 2020 has put a mirror up to all our faces. I spent twenty years of my life trying to navigate through not only my emotional blockages but being a business owner at the age of twenty-one, having a sick toddler at the age of twenty-three, and being in a toxic marriage at the age of twenty-five. Yet, my most significant moment of resilience comes from watching my three-year-old son beat cancer. He was diagnosed with medulloblastoma and spent two years of his life undergoing chemo and radiation.

AHYOKA YAMINA (LATISHA PRICE)

Lecturer, Morgan State University

I struggled as a young single mother because I was self-destructing and unconsciously trying to ignore the pain I felt by drinking, partying, and using illegal substances. It wasn't until my son got sick that I was forced to be strong. I had no choice; my son's life was on the line. I felt like I already wasted three years of his life running the streets, and my son's paternal grandmother was adamant about me being an unfit mother. I had to prove that I was stable enough to take on this task. Although I stepped up to the plate and matured as a mother, I still didn't deal with my trauma. Much of my twenties and thirties were filled with setback after setback. Until I reached the age of thirty-six and was divorcing my husband after twenty long, unfruitful years. It took for my sixteen-year-old son to have to intervene and prevent my ex from throwing me around our apartment like a rag doll for me to finally get it. My son has always been my earth angel, saving my life on numerous occasions.

That day, approximately four years ago, I decided that I wanted my life to change for me. I did a lot of growing during those years and learning about my spiritual gifts. Although, it took me four years to finally overcome my past as well as learn some new lessons. I did it! I found myself and my life's purpose. Everything I've experienced wasn't meant to break me but to help me heal other people like me. Who would have thought all those lessons would turn me into the Powerhouse I am today! I have completed my master's degree, working on my doctorate, full-time lecturer at one of the most prominent HBCU in the country, co-owner of a natural hair care salon, co-host of a leading talk show for entrepreneurs in Baltimore, and I have started my spiritual-based practice that has quickly expanded across the world.

AHYOKA YAMINA (LATISHA PRICE)
Lecturer, Morgan State University

Once you change the way you think and feel, your life changes for the better. I spent years in a low-vibrational frequency, trying to figure out why I couldn't manifest a great life. Heck, I was an awesome person to everyone. I remember thinking, why not me. Why do you keep skipping over me, God? Then the secret to my questions was revealed. I was trying to be everything to everyone but myself. But, once I turned that love inward, healed, changed my perspective about my life and self, practiced self-preservation, and maintained a happy vibration, the doors to the universe flew right open.

Who am I? I am an extension of the source. *I am Powerful! I am Loveable!* I am all that I say I am! If you don't gain anything else from my story, remember this: be gentle with yourself, and, most importantly, remember you are Loved! Allow your light to shine regardless. Accept who you are and be **POWERFUL!** Just follow your divine guidance, intuition, thoughts, and feelings. They are leading you toward your life's purpose.

WHAT DOES RESILIENCE . . .

FEEL LIKE?

1.

2.

3.

4.

SOUND LIKE?

_____
_____
_____
_____
_____

LOOK LIKE?

_____
_____
_____

WHAT'S ON MY MIND?

_____
_____
_____
_____
_____
_____
_____
_____
_____
_____
_____
_____
_____
_____
_____
_____
_____
_____
_____

"Never be afraid to sit awhile and think."
LORRAINE
HANSBERRY

MY EDUCATION GOAL(S)

- What is holding me back from achieving my education/skill goal(s)?
- What roadblocks to achieving my goal(s) are within my sphere of influence and control?

_____

_____

_____

_____

_____

_____

MY EDUCATION GOAL(S)

_____
_____
_____
_____
_____
_____
_____
_____
_____
_____
_____
_____
_____

MY CAREER
GOAL(S)

- What is holding me back from achieving my career goal(s)?
- What roadblocks to achieving my goal(s) are within my sphere of influence and control?

_____
_____
_____
_____
_____
_____

MY CAREER GOAL(S)

_____
_____
_____
_____
_____
_____
_____
_____
_____
_____
_____
_____
_____

LEGACY

MANINA BEALE-BUSH
Business Owner, Legacy BookBar

"What is your passion?" "What do you want to leave your kids when they grow up?" I have asked myself these questions for the past two years. I toyed around with a few ideas, and yet every time I changed my mind or stayed up late at night, I always had a book in hand. That's when I got a great idea to open a bookstore. After months of research, Legacy BookBar was born.

I was born and raised in Baltimore, Maryland, and I have three wonderful kids and a loving husband. Growing up, I watched my mom, dad, and maternal grandmother read book after book. They read everything from Stephen King's IT to John Henrik Clark's Christopher Columbus & the Afrikan Holocaust: Slavery & the Rise of European Capitalism. No subject was taboo or off-limits.

At the age of fifteen, I remember reading my first romance novel, and seeing people who looked like me on the cover was amazing. In 1995, I went to the mall with my mom to see if there were other novels written by people of color. When I couldn't find any, I asked the sales associate. She directed me to the back of the store. In deciding on what I wanted to do with my life, I remembered this story. We will no longer be shelved in the back of the store. Legacy BookBar is a place where people of color will shine bright through the entire store.

"DEFINING MYSELF, AS OPPOSED TO BEING DEFINED BY OTHERS, IS ONE OF THE MOST DIFFICULT CHALLENGES I FACE."

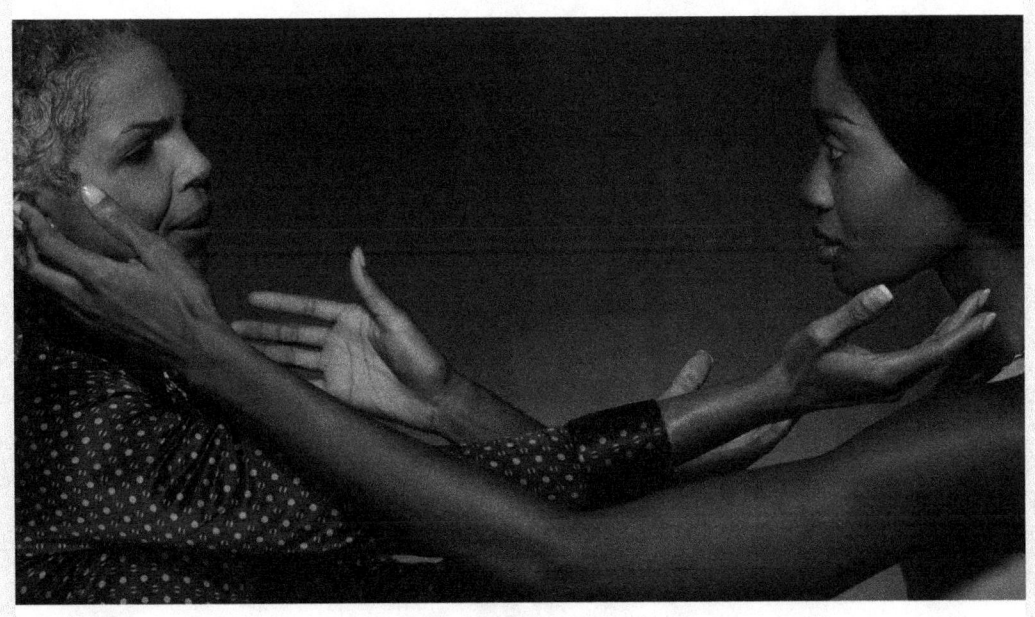

Carol Moseley Braun

The Woman in the Mirror

What Do I See?

How Well Do I Know Myself?

Strongly Disagree (1)
Disagree (2)
Neither Agree nor Disagree (3)
Agree (4)
Strongly Agree (5)

☐

I see a woman who knows her core values and their impact on her life.

☐

I see a woman who knows her strengths and areas of growth.

☐

I see a woman who understands the effect of white privilege and racism on her life.

☐

I see a woman who understands the effect of male privilege and sexism on her life.

☐

I see a woman who knows her purpose in life.

☐

I see a woman who knows how to manage her emotions effectively.

20/20 VISION

I AM

_____

_____

_____

I AM

_____

_____

_____

I AM

_____

_____

_____

_____

_____

_____

_____

_____

I AM . . . LOVING AND CURIOUS

NKOSAZANA KEMRAHA
Student, Towson University

I am loving and curious
I wonder about the people I encounter
I hear their thoughts floating above them
I see stars in the eyes of those I love
I want to grow and learn as I go along
I am loving and curious

I pretend that I am not easily troubled
I feel both solid and as if I could float away
I touch the delicate fabric of time
I worry about all that I have yet to accomplish
I cry for my younger self who lacked confidence
I am loving and curious

I understand that life is a journey to be enjoyed
I say pursue it all without hesitation
I dream of ocean waves and the journey ahead
I try to believe in the limitless potential inside me
I hope to live the life I know I deserve
I am loving and curious

20/20 VISION

I LOVE

_____
_____
_____

I LOVE

_____
_____
_____

I LOVE

_____
_____
_____
_____
_____
_____
_____

20/20 VISION

I DISLIKE

_____

_____

_____

I DISLIKE

_____

_____

_____

I DISLIKE

_____

_____

_____

_____

_____

_____

_____

_____

20/20 VISION

I WANT TO STOP

_____

_____

_____

I WANT TO STOP

_____

_____

_____

I WANT TO STOP

_____

_____

_____

_____

_____

_____

_____

WHAT'S ON MY MIND?

_____

_____

_____

_____

_____

_____

_____

_____

_____

_____

_____

_____

_____

_____

"Never be afraid to sit awhile and think."

LORRAINE HANSBERRY

HEART'S CANVAS

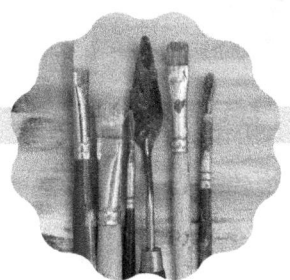

20/20 VISION

I WANT TO CONTINUE

_____
_____
_____

I WANT TO CONTINUE

_____
_____
_____

I WANT TO CONTINUE

_____
_____
_____
_____
_____
_____
_____

20/20 VISION

I WANT TO BEGIN

_____
_____
_____

I WANT TO BEGIN

_____
_____
_____

I WANT TO BEGIN

_____
_____
_____
_____
_____
_____

APTITUDES, INTERESTS, & STRENGTHS

At Work

APTITUDES:
A natural ability or talent

INTERESTS:
Something or someone that sparks attention

STRENGTHS:
Skills, knowledge, talents, and proficiencies that are learned

APTITUDES, INTERESTS, & STRENGTHS

At School

APTITUDES:
A natural ability or talent

INTERESTS:
Something or someone that sparks attention

STRENGTHS:
Skills, knowledge, talents, and proficiencies that are learned

JANELLE MONAE

"Embrace what makes you unique, even if it makes others uncomfortable. I didn't have to become perfect because I've learned throughout my journey that perfection is the enemy of greatness."

VALUES LIST

Acceptance
Accomplishment
Accountability
Achievement
Adaptability
Altruism
Ambition
Assertiveness
Balance
Beauty
Boldness
Challenge
Charity
Cleanliness
Comfort
Commitment
Common sense
Communication
Community
Compassion
Competence
Confidence
Connection
Consciousness
Consistency
Contentment
Contribution
Control
Conviction
Cooperation
Courage
Courtesy
Creation
Creativity

Credibility
Curiosity
Decisiveness
Dedication
Dependability
Determination
Devotion
Dignity
Discipline
Drive
Effectiveness
Efficiency
Empathy
Empowerment
Endurance
Enjoyment
Enthusiasm
Equality
Ethical
Excellence
Exploration
Fairness
Family
Fearless
Feelings
Fidelity
Focus
Foresight
Fortitude
Freedom
Friendship
Fun
Generosity
Genius

Giving
Goodness
Grace
Gratitude
Greatness
Growth
Happiness
Hard work
Harmony
Health
Honesty
Honor
Hope
Humility
Humor
Imagination
Improvement
Independence
Individuality
Innovation
Inquisitive
Insight
Integrity
Intelligence
Intuition
Joy
Justice
Kindness
Knowledge
Lawful
Leadership
Learning
Liberty
Logic

VALUES LIST

Love	Rigor	Trust
Loyalty	Risk	Truth
Mastery	Security	Understanding
Maturity	Self-reliance	Uniqueness
Meaning	Selfless	Unity
Motivation	Sensitivity	Valor
Openness	Serenity	Victory
Optimism	Service	Vigor
Order	Sharing	Vision
Organization	Sincerity	Vitality
Originality	Skill	Wealth
Passion	Smart	Winning
Patience	Spirituality	Wisdom
Peace	Stability	Wonder
Performance	Status	
Persistence	Stewardship	
Playfulness	Strength	**ADD MY OWN**
Poise	Success	
Potential	Support	_____
Power	Sustainability	
Productivity	Talent	_____
Professionalism	Teamwork	
Prosperity	Temperance	_____
Purpose	Thankful	
Reason	Thorough	_____
Recognition	Thoughtful	
Recreation	Timeliness	_____
Respect	Tolerance	
Responsibility	Toughness	_____
Restraint	Traditional	
Results-oriented	Tranquility	_____
Reverence	Transparency	
		_____

CORE VALUES

MY TOP 10

1.

2.

3.

4.

5.

6.

7.

8.

9.

10.

MY TOP 5

_____

_____

_____

_____

MY TOP 3

_____

_____

_____

WHAT'S ON MY MIND?

_____
_____
_____
_____
_____
_____
_____
_____
_____
_____
_____
_____
_____
_____
_____
_____

"Never be afraid to sit awhile and think."
LORRAINE
HANSBERRY

MY FINANCIAL GOAL(S)

- What is holding me back from achieving my financial goal(s)?
- What roadblocks to achieving my goal(s) are within my sphere of influence and control?

MY FINANCIAL GOAL(S)

_____
_____
_____
_____
_____
_____
_____
_____
_____
_____
_____
_____
_____

"MY MISSION IN LIFE IS NOT MERELY TO SURVIVE, BUT TO THRIVE; AND TO DO SO WITH SOME PASSION, SOME COMPASSION, SOME HUMOR, AND SOME STYLE."

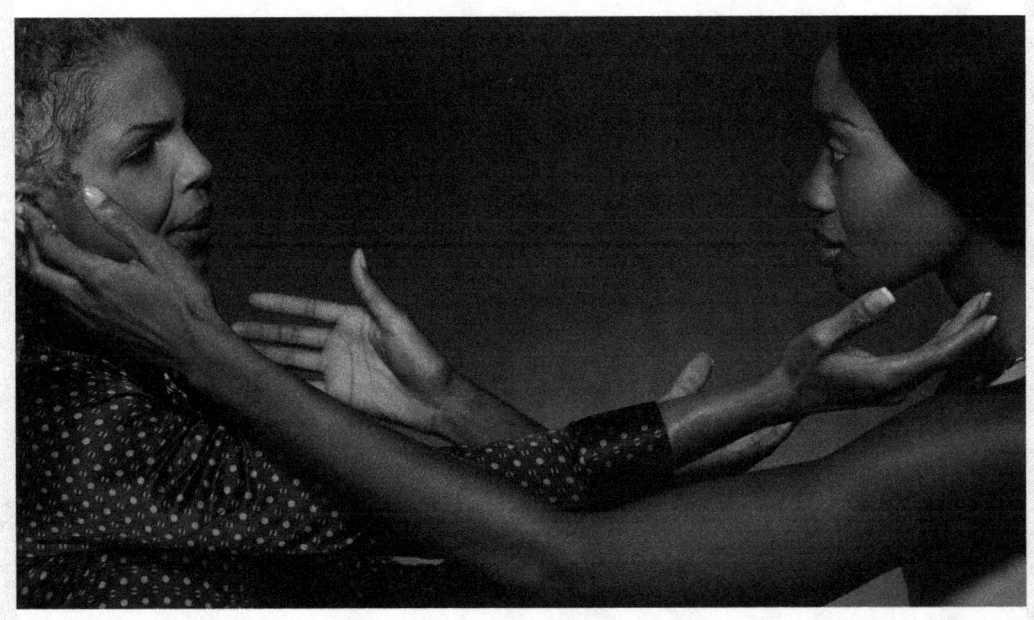

Maya Angelou

The Woman
with Heart

What Do I Feel?

FEELINGS: FOR BETTER AND FOR WORSE

What I was taught about feelings (emotions)

_____
_____
_____
_____
_____
_____

What I believe about feelings (emotions)

_____
_____
_____
_____
_____
_____
_____

FEELINGS: FOR BETTER AND FOR WORSE

What I want to know about my feelings (emotions)

_____

_____

_____

_____

_____

_____

Lessons I've learned about my feelings (emotions)

_____

_____

_____

_____

_____

_____

_____

SIMONE BILES

"I'd rather regret the risks that didn't work out than the chances I didn't take at all."

ANGER

CONTEMPT

DISGUST

BASIC
EMOTIONS

FEAR

HAPPINESS

SADNESS

surprise

Source: PaulEkmanGroup (2020)

WHAT MY FACIAL EXPRESSIONS
REVEAL ABOUT WHAT I AM FEELING

MY PHYSICAL RESPONSES
TO BASIC EMOTIONS

Facial expression, Body language, Tone of voice

EMOTIONAL TRIGGERS

Opinions, words, and situations can trigger an emotional response. Emotional triggers can be external and internal..

3 REASONS FOR EMOTIONAL TRIGGERS

✓ When your belief and/or values are in opposition to someone else's

✓ When you've experienced a traumatic event in your life

Source: Luna, A., *How to Identify Your Emotional Triggers (Before It's Too Late)* (2021)

✓ When you seek to preserve your ego

EMOTIONAL TRIGGERS

Emotional triggers can occur when one or more important needs and desires are not met or are challenged, such as the following:

Acceptance
Autonomy
Attention
Consistency
Fun
Love
Peacefulness
Predictability
Respect
Safety
Being liked
Being needed
Being right
Being treated fairly
Being valued

Source: Luna, A., *How to Identify Your Emotional Triggers (Before It's Too Late)* (2021)

EMOTIONAL TRIGGERS

ANGER

CONTEMPT

DISGUST

EMOTIONAL TRIGGERS

FEAR

HAPPINESS

EMOTIONAL TRIGGERS

SURPRISE

SADNESS

MY TOP 5 EMOTIONAL TRIGGERS

1

2

3

4

5

100

WHAT'S ON MY MIND?

_____
_____
_____
_____
_____
_____
_____
_____
_____
_____
_____
_____
_____

"Never be afraid to sit awhile and think."

LORRAINE
HANSBERRY

FIGHT, GIRL, FIGHT

KT ALARK
Mental and Public Health Professional

FIGHT like Your Life Depends on it! FIGHT like you have a destiny to fulfill! FIGHT like you are your ancestors' Wildest Dreams!

FIGHT, GIRL, FIGHT

How do you fight when the marriage you prayed and fasted for ends? How do you fight breast cancer when you are emotionally drained from your marriage ending? How do you fight when your entire world seemingly collapses?

HOW DO YOU FIGHT?

PRAY

God, help me. How did I get here? Why me, God? God, help me to survive all of this. Help me not to define myself by a failed marriage. Heal my heart that hurts and my spirit that is broken. Heal my body because I have to parent the gift you have given me in my child. God, help me to feel your love and not be fearful. God, help me to believe that you do all things well and that all of this is working for my good.

BELIEVE

What do you believe when hell is happening all around you? That I am ultimately going to be okay. Because I still have a lot to live for. I still need to nurture my son into greatness. I still need to experience love. I still need to tell my story. God, no matter what it looks like, I still believe in you! So I wake up every morning with tears and fear in my eyes and say, "I believe I am going to survive!" Why could I believe? With all my flaws and brokenness, God's love and mercy are made sufficient in me.

BECOME

After three years, one divorce, two surgeries, four rounds of radiation, eight mammograms, loss of finances, downsizing to an apartment, the sudden death of a best friend, loss of friendships, and countless tears, I have BECOME a woman of promise, love, peace, and destiny. The ancestral of women before are cheering me on, and I have **BECOME** so much more than they ever dreamed. Because God made me fearfully and wonderfully. Hence, I am *STRONG*, and *I SURVIVED*. And so can *YOU!*

FIGHT, GIRL, FIGHT

MY MINDSET GOAL(S)

- What is holding me back from achieving my mindset goal(s)?
- What roadblocks to achieving my goal(s) are within my sphere of influence and control?

_____

_____

_____

_____

_____

_____

MY MINDSET GOAL(S)

_____

_____

_____

_____

_____

_____

_____

_____

_____

_____

_____

_____

"DON'T LET ANYONE STEAL YA JOY! THERE'S ALWAYS SOMEONE MISERABLE TRYING TO BRING YOU DOWN ... YOU JUST WISH THEM WELL & PROCEED ON ENJOYING YOUR LIFE."

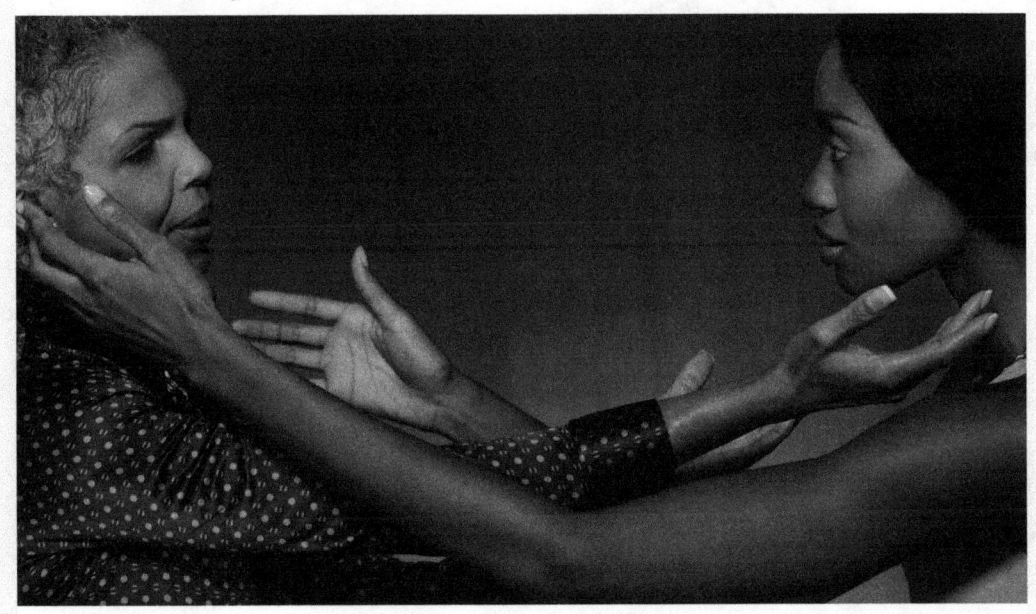

Missy Elliott

The Woman with Helping Hands

What Can I Build?

WHAT COMMUNITY MEANS
TO ME

_____
_____
_____
_____
_____
_____
_____
_____
_____
_____
_____
_____
_____
_____
_____
_____
_____
_____

MY COMMUNITIES

Family, friends, social networks, professional
associations, athletic leagues, etc.

Communities I feel comfortable and accepted

Communities I feel less comfortable and/or unaccepted

_____

_____

_____

_____

Communities I would like to join or learn more about

MY ALLIES

Allies are like air, water, and food—essential for survival.

HOME

WORK AND/OR
SCHOOL

COMMUNITY
(People and/or
Organizations)

A TIME WHEN MY UNIQUENESS WAS NOT ACCEPTED, VALUED, AND/OR SUPPORTED

_____

_____

_____

_____

_____

_____

_____

_____

_____

_____

_____

WHAT I NEED TO FEEL ACCEPTED, VALUED, AND SUPPORTED

HOME

WORK AND/OR SCHOOL

COMMUNITY
(People and/or Organizations)

A TIME WHEN MY UNIQUENESS WAS ACCEPTED, VALUED, AND/OR SUPPORTED

_____

_____

_____

_____

_____

_____

_____

_____

_____

_____

_____

_____

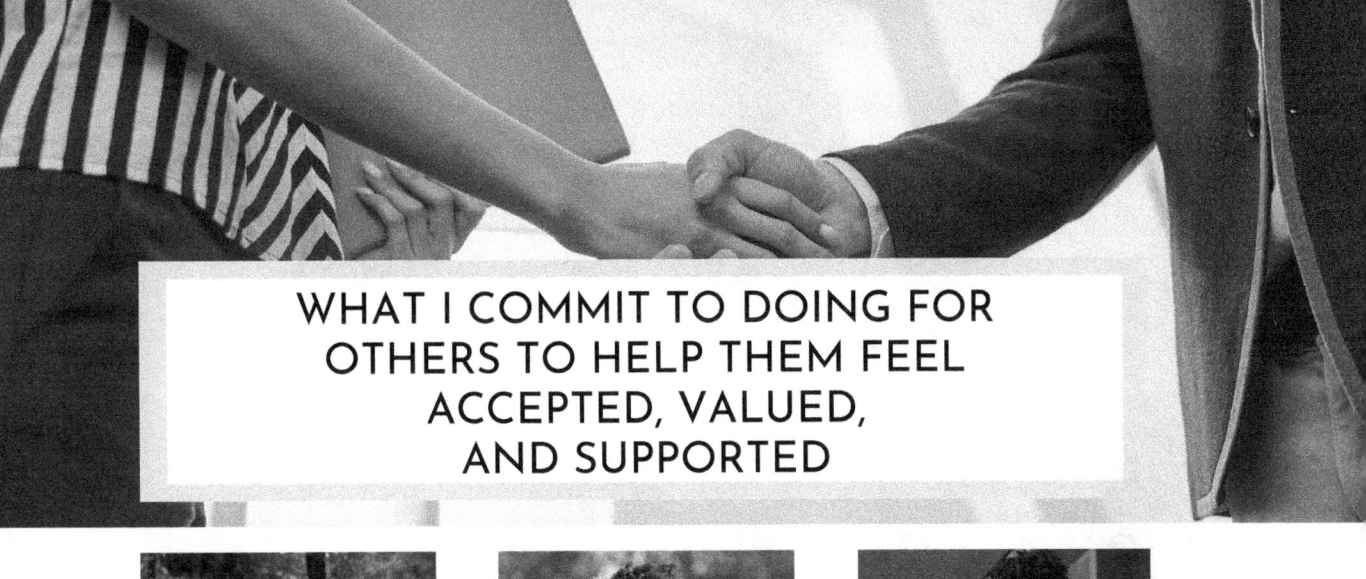

WHAT I COMMIT TO DOING FOR OTHERS TO HELP THEM FEEL ACCEPTED, VALUED, AND SUPPORTED

HOME

WORK AND/OR SCHOOL

COMMUNITY
(People and/or Organizations)

WHAT'S ON MY MIND?

_____
_____
_____
_____
_____
_____
_____
_____
_____
_____
_____
_____
_____
_____
_____
_____
_____

*"Never be afraid to sit awhile
and think."*

LORRAINE
HANSBERRY

MY PUBLIC SERVICE GOAL(S)

- What is holding me back from achieving my public service goal(s)?
- What can I do to alter or improve my mindset or attitude to achieve my goal(s)?

_____

_____

_____

_____

_____

_____

MY PUBLIC SERVICE GOAL(S)

_____
_____
_____
_____
_____
_____
_____
_____
_____
_____
_____
_____
_____
_____

WHAT DOES TRUST . . .

LOOK LIKE?

1.

2.

3.

4.

SOUND LIKE?

_____

_____

_____

_____

FEEL LIKE?

_____

_____

_____

118

HOW I CAN BUILD AND/OR REINFORCE TRUST IN MY COMMUNITIES

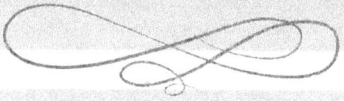

MY FAMILY GOAL(S)

- What is holding me back from achieving my family goal(s)?
- What roadblocks to achieving my goal(s) are within my sphere of influence and control?

_____
_____
_____
_____
_____
_____

MY FAMILY GOAL(S)

"CARING FOR MYSELF IS NOT SELF-INDULGENCE, IT IS SELF-PRESERVATION, AND THAT IS AN ACT OF POLITICAL WARFARE."

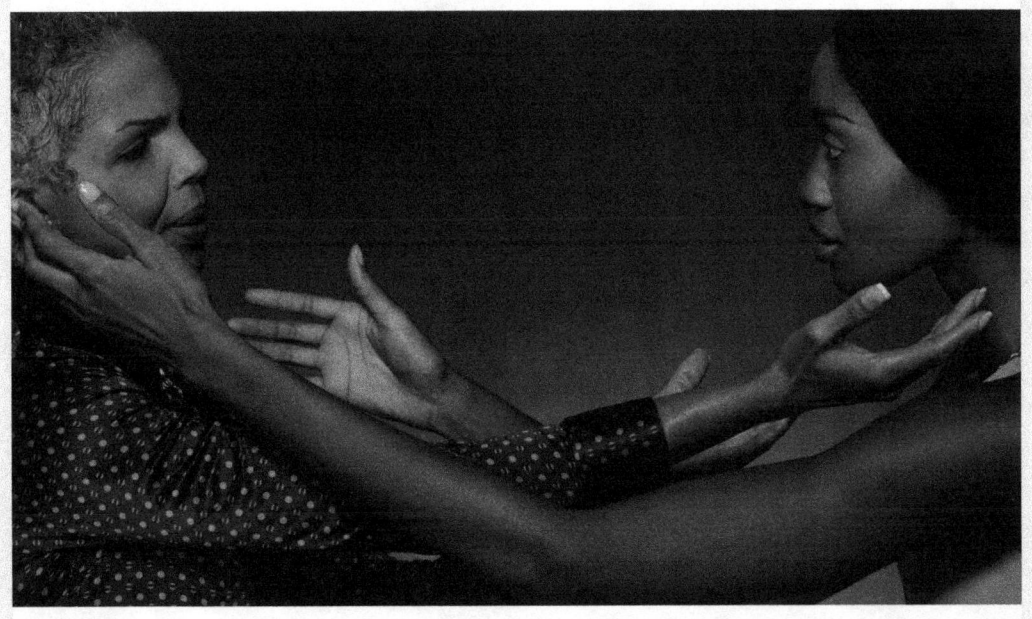

Audre Lorde

The Woman of Good Health

How Do I Care for Myself?

TAKING CARE OF THE WHOLE ME IS SELF-CARE

"The more we practice deliberately caring for our well-being, the more resilient we become, which ultimately helps strengthen our ability to cope with and manage whatever comes our way in life."

SELF-CARE IS NOT A SIGN OF WEAKNESS, SELFISHNESS OR

the same for everyone.

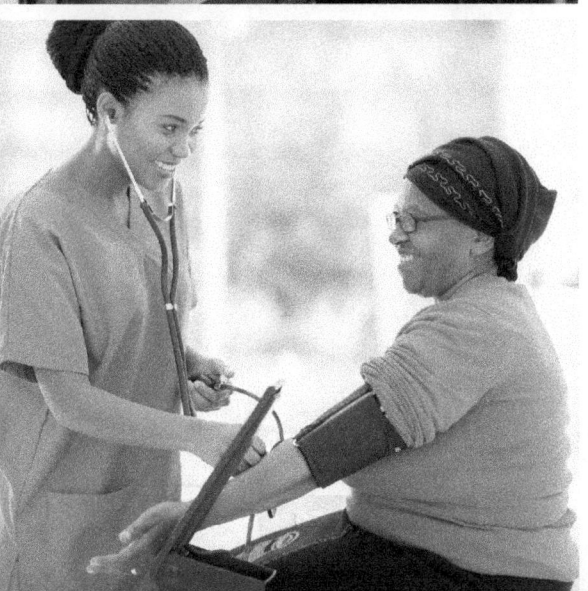

SELF-CARE IS NECESSARY, INTENTIONAL, EVER-CHANGING AND AN EXAMPLE OF

Self-love and compassion

Source: Suleman, K. (2019) Mental Health Match

FORMS OF SELF-CARE

EMOTIONAL

MENTAL

PHYSICAL

PRACTICAL

PROFESSIONAL

RELATIONAL

SPIRITUAL

MY SELF-CARE CHECKUP

Low (L)
Average (A)
High (H)
Maximum (M)

☐ **Emotional wellbeing:** I engage in activities that help me explore, understand, and manage my emotions.

☐ **Mental wellbeing:** I engage in activities that help me calm my mind and reduce stress.

☐ **Physical wellbeing:** I engage in activities that help me maintain a healthy body.

just breathe

☐ **Practical wellbeing:** I engage in activities that help me meet my core needs.

☐ **Professional wellbeing:** I engage in activities that help me be engaged, fulfilled, qualified, and safe.

☐ **Relational wellbeing:** I engage in activities that help me connect with those I care about and who cares about me.

LEVEL UP

☐ **Spiritual wellbeing:** I engage in activities (religious or non-religious) that help me nurture my soul and have a higher purpose than self.

MY SELF-CARE
CHECKUP

Low (L)
Average (A)
High (H)
Maximum (M)

☐ I get enough sleep, rest, and relaxation to recharge my mind and body.

☐ I engage in regular physical activities that aid in movement, endurance, and strength.

GOAL
Getter

☐ I eat healthy, balanced meals everyday--plenty of fruits, vegetables, and water.

☐ I maintain a work-life balance.

☐ I increase my knowledge and skills, and cultivate my talents.

☐ I foster positive, affirming relationships with family, friends, and colleagues.

**GAME
ON**

☐ I live a life of purpose and meaning--engaging in passion projects and works.

SELF-CARE EXAMPLES

EMOTIONAL

- Share/post only positive things on social media
- Refrain from being overly critical of self
- Declutter your living or work space

MENTAL

- Challenge negative thinking
- Reduce amount of time spent on social media/technology
- Avoid toxic people
- Begin a new hobby

PHYSICAL

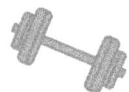

- Drink plenty of water
- Exercise regularly
- Get 8 hours of sleep
- Reduce sugar and salt intake

PRACTICAL

- Create a household budget
- Take a professional learning course
- Get regular health exams
- Talk to a therapist

PROFESSIONAL

- Take lunch breaks
- Use vacation and sick days
- Assume positive intentions from colleagues

RELATIONAL

- Have a monthly date night
- Call family/friend weekly
- Listen with empathy

SPIRITUAL

- Practice deep breathing exercises
- Meditate daily
- Take yoga classes

WHAT'S ON MY MIND?

_____

_____

_____

_____

_____

_____

_____

_____

_____

_____

_____

_____

_____

_____

"Never be afraid to sit awhile and think."

LORRAINE HANSBERRY

MY PHYSICAL GOAL(S)

- What is holding me back from achieving my physical goal(s)?
- What roadblocks to achieving my goal(s) are within my sphere of influence and control?

MY PHYSICAL GOAL(S)

_____
_____
_____
_____
_____
_____
_____
_____
_____
_____
_____
_____
_____
_____

A WEEK OF SELF-CARE

New Self-Care Activities

Goal:

Steps I will take to achieve my goal:

A WEEK OF SELF-CARE

New Self-Care Activities

Goal:

Steps I will take to achieve my goal:

MY WEEK OF
SELF-CARE ACTIVITIES

MONDAY

TUESDAY

WEDNESDAY

THURSDAY

FRIDAY

WEEKEND

MY WEEK OF
SELF-CARE ACTIVITIES

MONDAY

TUESDAY

WEDNESDAY

THURSDAY

FRIDAY

WEEKEND

MY WEEK OF SELF-CARE

REFLECTION

_____
_____
_____
_____
_____
_____
_____
_____
_____
_____
_____
_____
_____
_____

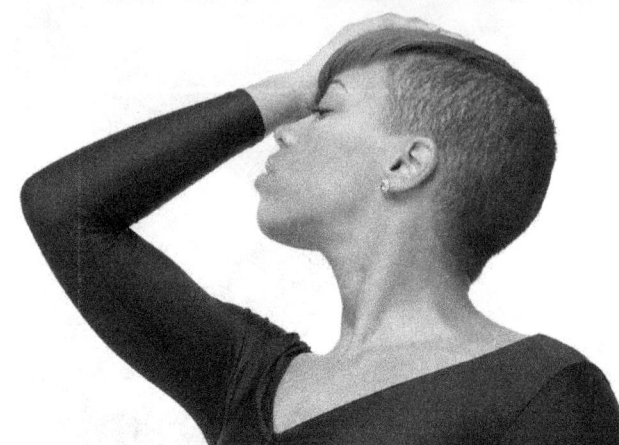

MY WEEK OF SELF-CARE

REFLECTION

_____

_____

_____

_____

_____

_____

_____

_____

_____

_____

_____

_____

_____

_____

MY PLEASURE
GOAL(S)

- What is holding me back from achieving my pleasure/enjoyment goal(s)?
- What roadblocks to achieving my goal(s) are within my sphere of influence and control?

_____

_____

_____

_____

_____

_____

MY PLEASURE
GOAL(S)

_____
_____
_____
_____
_____
_____
_____
_____
_____
_____
_____
_____
_____

A Month

of Joy

Activities for my self-love month of joy

DATE   ACTIVITY

_____

_____

_____

_____

_____

_____

_____

_____

_____

_____

A Month
of Joy

Activities for my self-love month of joy

DATE   ACTIVITY

_____

_____

_____

_____

_____

_____

_____

_____

MY MONTH OF JOY

REFLECTION

_____
_____
_____
_____
_____
_____
_____
_____
_____
_____
_____

MY MONTH OF JOY

REFLECTION

_____

_____

_____

_____

_____

_____

_____

_____

_____

_____

_____

PART 2
JOURNAL

PEBBLES
&
BOULDERS

It's important to name and claim the small and big challenges you face. Then ask yourself: Of these challenges, which ones are in my sphere of control?

PEBBLES
&
BOULDERS

PEBBLES
&
BOULDERS

PEBBLES
&
BOULDERS

PEBBLES
&
BOULDERS

PEBBLES
&
BOULDERS

PEBBLES
&
BOULDERS

PEBBLES
&
BOULDERS

PEBBLES & BOULDERS

PEBBLES
&
BOULDERS

PEBBLES
&
BOULDERS

'NUFF SAID

There are times when a word, phrase, or sentence is enough.

'NUFF SAID

_____
_____
_____

_____
_____
_____

_____
_____
_____

_____
_____

'NUFF SAID

'NUFF SAID

_____

_____

_____

_____

_____

_____

_____

_____

_____

_____

_____

'NUFF SAID

_____

_____

_____

_____

_____

_____

_____

_____

_____

'NUFF SAID

_____
_____
_____

_____
_____
_____

_____
_____
_____

_____
_____

'NUFF SAID

'NUFF SAID

_____

_____

_____

_____

_____

_____

_____

_____

_____

_____

_____

'NUFF SAID

'NUFF SAID

_____
_____
_____

_____
_____
_____

_____
_____
_____

_____
_____

'NUFF SAID

_____

_____

_____

_____

_____

_____

_____

_____

_____

_____

_____

FORGET ME NOT

Don't forget to appreciate what makes you smile, laugh, cheer, even cry tears of joy.

FORGET ME NOT

FORGET ME NOT

FORGET ME NOT

FORGET ME NOT

_____
_____
_____
_____
_____
_____
_____
_____
_____
_____
_____
_____
_____
_____
_____
_____

FORGET ME NOT

FORGET ME NOT

FORGET ME NOT

FORGET ME NOT

FORGET ME NOT

_____

_____

_____

_____

_____

_____

_____

_____

_____

_____

_____

_____

_____

_____

_____

_____

_____

_____

_____

_____

FORGET ME NOT

HEART'S
CANVAS

Where words
sometimes fail,
drawing from the
heart rarely does.

HEART'S CANVAS

HEART'S CANVAS

HEART'S CANVAS

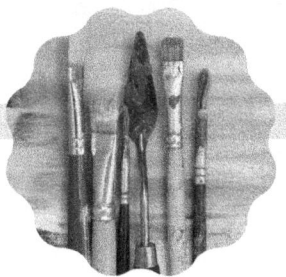

HEART'S CANVAS

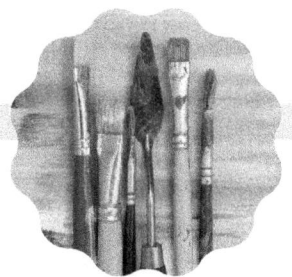

HEART'S CANVAS

HEART'S CANVAS

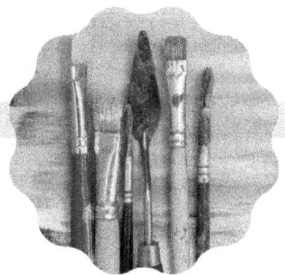

HEART'S CANVAS

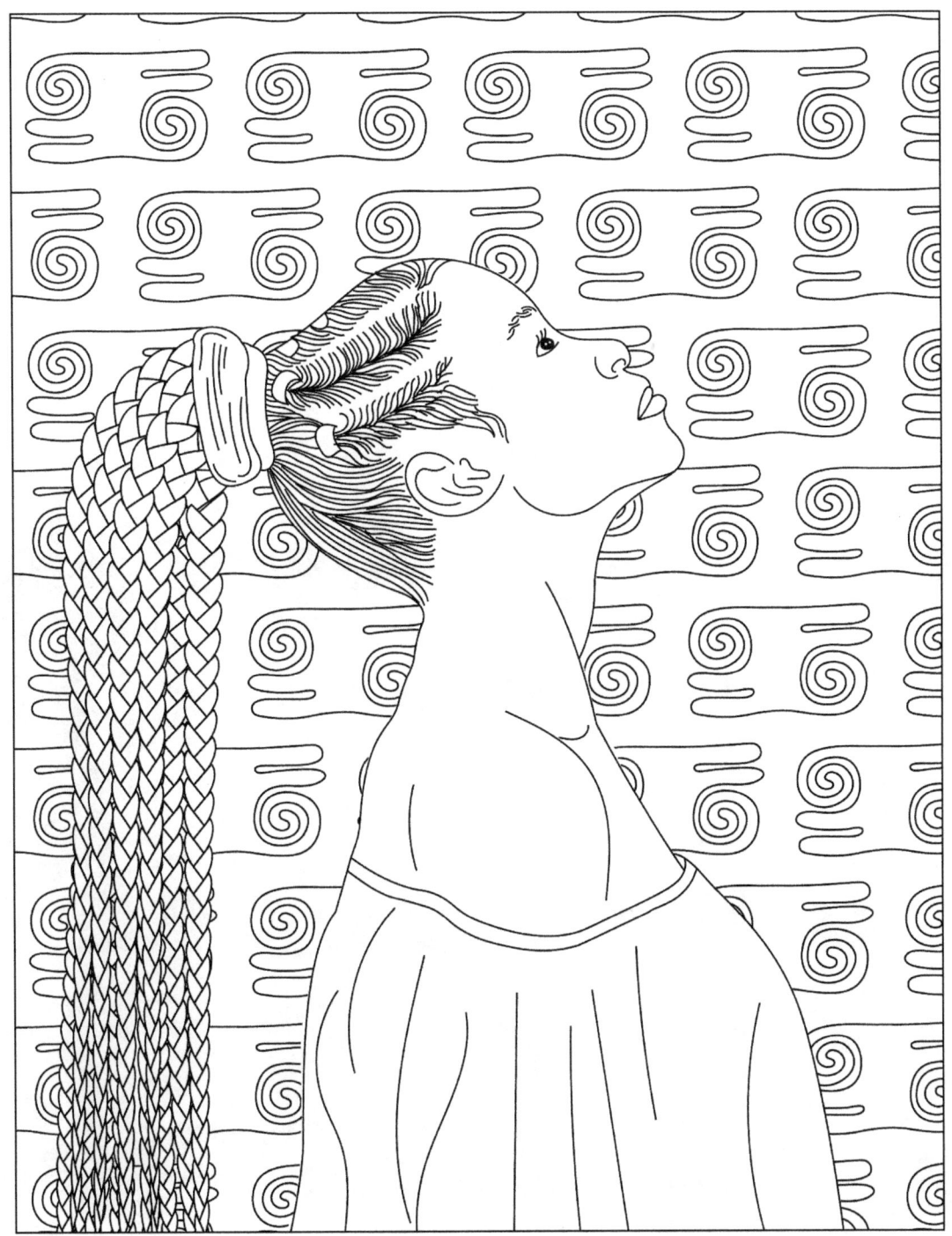

188

NO POSTAGE NECESSARY

All letters don't have to be sent, but certain letters are worth writing.

195

NO POSTAGE NECESSARY

Acceptance
Anger
Belonging
Caring
Compassion
Envy
Desire
Disgust
Distrust
Fear
Fidelity
Friendship
Gratitude
Greed
Guilt
Happiness
Hate

Hopefulness
Hopelessness
Hurt
Impatience
Insecurity
Intolerance
Jealousy
Kindness
Love
Possessive
Pride
Protective
Regret
Respect
Sadness
Shame
Trust

NO POSTAGE NECESSARY

Colleague
Doctor
Father
Friend
Grandparent
Mother
Neighbor
Offspring
Partner

Police Officer
Sibling
Spiritual/Religious
Leader
Spouse
Stranger
Supervisor
Teacher

NO POSTAGE NECESSARY

Dear

NO POSTAGE
NECESSARY

Dear

_____

_____

_____

_____

_____

_____

_____

_____

_____

_____

_____

_____

_____

_____

_____

_____

_____

NO POSTAGE
NECESSARY

Dear

_____

_____

_____

_____

_____

_____

_____

_____

_____

_____

_____

_____

_____

_____

_____

_____

_____

_____

NO POSTAGE NECESSARY

Dear

_____

_____

_____

_____

_____

_____

_____

_____

_____

_____

_____

_____

_____

_____

_____

_____

_____

NO POSTAGE NECESSARY

Dear

_____

_____

_____

_____

_____

_____

_____

_____

_____

_____

_____

_____

_____

_____

_____

_____

NO POSTAGE NECESSARY

Dear

_____

_____

_____

_____

_____

_____

_____

_____

_____

_____

_____

_____

_____

_____

NO POSTAGE NECESSARY

Dear

_____

_____

_____

_____

_____

_____

_____

_____

_____

_____

_____

_____

_____

_____

_____

_____

_____

NO POSTAGE NECESSARY

Dear

_____

_____

_____

_____

_____

_____

_____

_____

_____

_____

_____

_____

_____

_____

_____

_____

_____

_____

_____

NO POSTAGE NECESSARY

Dear

_____

_____

_____

_____

_____

_____

_____

_____

_____

_____

_____

_____

_____

_____

_____

_____

_____

_____

_____

NO POSTAGE NECESSARY

Dear

_____

_____

_____

_____

_____

_____

_____

_____

_____

_____

_____

_____

_____

_____

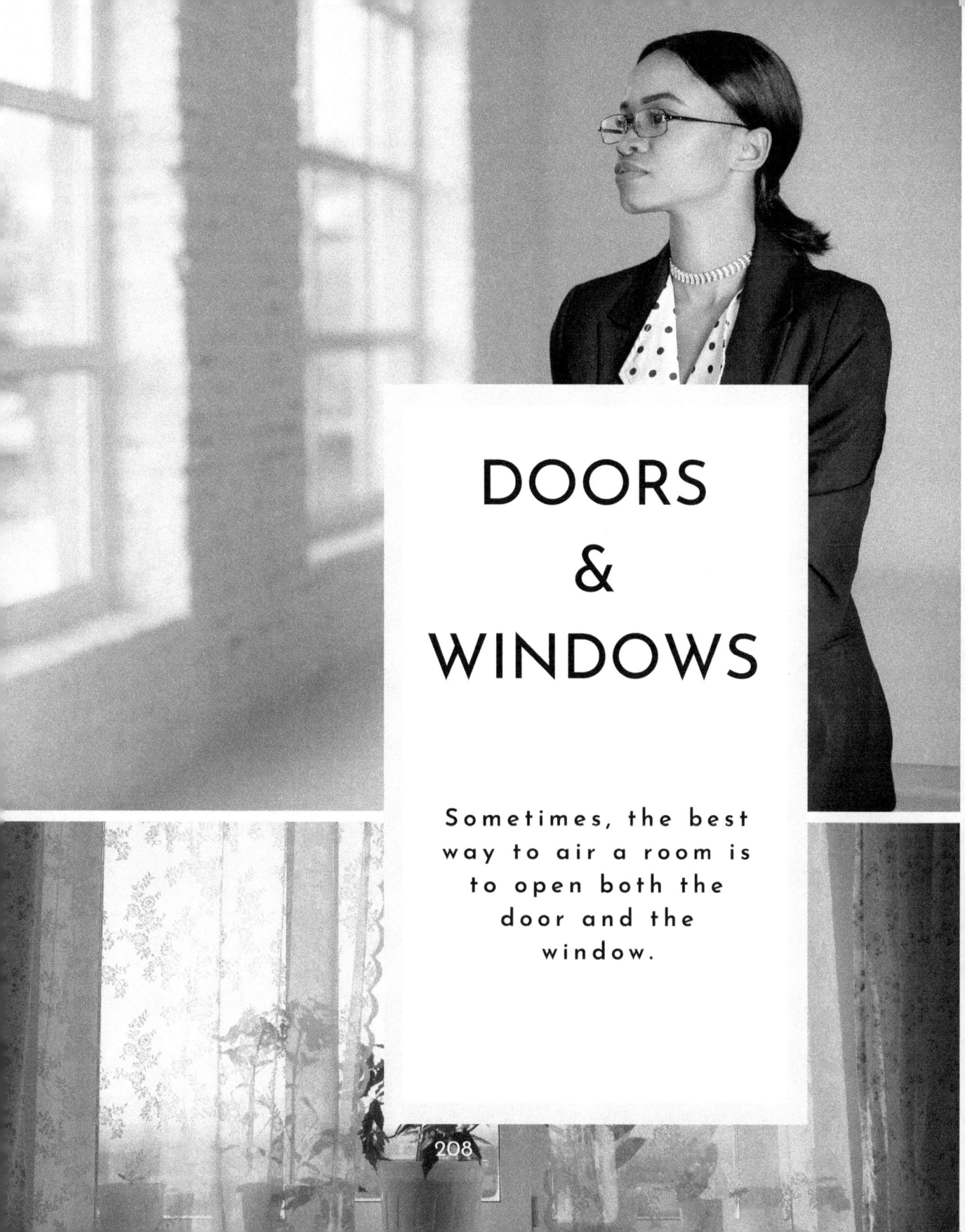

DOORS
&
WINDOWS

Sometimes, the best way to air a room is to open both the door and the window.

DOORS & WINDOWS

Ableism
Abortion
Aging
Anger
Birth Control
Bullying
Childhood
Affirmative Action
Black Lives Matter Movement
Child Marriage
Classism
Contempt
COVID-19
Cultural Identity Abuse
Dating
Death
Discrimination
Disgust
Divorce
Drug/Alcohol Abuse
Education
Emotional/Verbal Abuse

Employment
Fear
Female Genital Mutilation
Financial/Economic Abuse
Gender Equality
Gender Identity
Gun Control
Happiness
Homophobia
Justice System
Infidelity
Law Enforcement
Marriage
Menopause
Mental/Psychological Abuse
Mental Health
Midlife Crisis
Motherhood
Obesity
Parenting
Physical Abuse
Physical Health

Police Brutality
Political Parties
Prejudice
Prison
Protests
Race
Racism
Redlining
Religion
Reparations
Reproductive Rights
Romantic Relationships
Sadness
Sex
Sex Trafficking
Sexism
Sexual Abuse
Sexuality
Sickness/Illness
Spirituality
Suicide
Teen Pregnancy
Violence
Voting

DOORS
&
WINDOWS

_____
_____
_____
_____
_____
_____
_____
_____
_____
_____
_____
_____
_____
_____
_____
_____

DOORS
&
WINDOWS

DOORS
&
WINDOWS

_____
_____
_____
_____
_____
_____
_____
_____
_____
_____
_____
_____
_____
_____
_____
_____
_____

DOORS
&
WINDOWS

_____
_____
_____
_____
_____
_____
_____
_____
_____
_____
_____
_____
_____
_____
_____
_____

DOORS
&
WINDOWS

_____
_____
_____
_____
_____
_____
_____
_____
_____
_____
_____
_____
_____
_____
_____
_____

DOORS
&
WINDOWS

_____
_____
_____
_____
_____
_____
_____
_____
_____
_____
_____
_____
_____
_____
_____
_____
_____

DOORS
&
WINDOWS

_____
_____
_____
_____
_____
_____
_____
_____
_____
_____
_____
_____
_____
_____
_____
_____
_____

DOORS
&
WINDOWS

_____

_____

_____

_____

_____

_____

_____

_____

_____

_____

_____

_____

_____

_____

_____

_____

DOORS
&
WINDOWS

DOORS
&
WINDOWS

DOORS
&
WINDOWS

_____
_____
_____
_____
_____
_____
_____
_____
_____
_____
_____
_____
_____
_____
_____
_____
_____
_____

PART 3
LEVEL UP

WHAT'S MY WHY?

_____

_____

_____

_____

_____

_____

_____

_____

_____

_____

_____

_____

_____

_____

_____

WHAT'S MY WHY?

_____

_____

_____

_____

_____

_____

_____

_____

_____

_____

_____

_____

_____

_____

_____

_____

_____

WHAT'S MY WHY?

_____

_____

_____

_____

_____

_____

_____

_____

_____

_____

_____

_____

_____

_____

_____

_____

WHAT'S MY WHY?

_____

_____

_____

_____

_____

_____

_____

_____

_____

_____

_____

_____

_____

_____

_____

_____

_____

MY CAREER GOAL(S)

- What is holding me back from achieving my career goal(s)?
- What roadblocks to achieving my goal(s) are within my sphere of influence and control?

_____
_____
_____
_____
_____
_____

MY CAREER GOAL(S)

_____
_____
_____
_____
_____
_____
_____
_____
_____
_____
_____
_____
_____
_____

MY EDUCATION GOAL(S)

- What is holding me back from achieving my education/skill goal(s)?
- What roadblocks to achieving my goal(s) are within my sphere of influence and control?

_____
_____
_____
_____
_____
_____

MY EDUCATION GOAL(S)

_____
_____
_____
_____
_____
_____
_____
_____
_____
_____
_____
_____
_____

MY FAMILY GOAL(S)

- What is holding me back from achieving my family goal(s)?
- What roadblocks to achieving my goal(s) are within my sphere of influence and control?

_____

_____

_____

_____

_____

MY FAMILY
GOAL(S)

_____

_____

_____

_____

_____

_____

_____

_____

_____

_____

_____

_____

_____

MY FINANCIAL GOAL(S)

- What is holding me back from achieving my financial goal(s)?
- What roadblocks to achieving my goal(s) are within my sphere of influence and control?

_____

_____

_____

_____

_____

_____

MY FINANCIAL GOAL(S)

_____
_____
_____
_____
_____
_____
_____
_____
_____
_____
_____
_____
_____
_____

MY MINDSET GOAL(S)

- What is holding me back from achieving my mindset goal(s)?
- What roadblocks to achieving my goal(s) are within my sphere of influence and control?

_____

_____

_____

_____

_____

_____

MY MINDSET GOAL(S)

_____
_____
_____
_____
_____
_____
_____
_____
_____
_____
_____
_____

MY PHYSICAL GOAL(S)

- What is holding me back from achieving my physical goal(s)?
- What roadblocks to achieving my goal(s) are within my sphere of influence and control?

_____

_____

_____

_____

_____

_____

MY PHYSICAL
GOAL(S)

_____

_____

_____

_____

_____

_____

_____

_____

_____

_____

_____

MY PLEASURE
GOAL(S)

- What is holding me back from achieving my pleasure/enjoyment goal(s)?
- What roadblocks to achieving my goal(s) are within my sphere of influence and control?

_____
_____
_____
_____
_____
_____

MY PLEASURE
GOAL(S)

_____
_____
_____
_____
_____
_____
_____
_____
_____
_____
_____
_____
_____

MY PUBLIC SERVICE GOAL(S)

- What is holding me back from achieving my public service goal(s)?
- What can I do to alter or improve my mindset or attitude to achieve my goal(s)?

_____
_____
_____
_____
_____
_____

MY PUBLIC SERVICE GOAL(S)

_____
_____
_____
_____
_____
_____
_____
_____
_____
_____
_____
_____
_____
_____

WHAT DOES RESILIENCE . . .

FEEL LIKE?

1.

2.

3.

4.

SOUND LIKE?

_____
_____
_____
_____
_____

LOOK LIKE?

_____
_____

242

WHAT DOES RESILIENCE . . .

FEEL LIKE?

1.

2.

3.

4.

SOUND LIKE?

_____

_____

_____

_____

_____

LOOK LIKE?

_____

_____

How Well Do I Know Myself?

Strongly Disagree (1)
Disagree (2)
Neither Agree nor Disagree (3)
Agree (4)
Strongly Agree (5)

☐

I see a woman who knows her core values and their impact on her life.

☐

I see a woman who knows her strengths and areas of growth.

☐

I see a woman who understands the effect of white privilege and racism on her life.

☐

I see a woman who understands the effect of male privilege and sexism on her life.

☐

I see a woman who knows her purpose in life.

☐

I see a woman who knows how to manage her emotions effectively.

How Well Do I Know Myself?

Strongly Disagree (1)
Disagree (2)
Neither Agree nor Disagree (3)
Agree (4)
Strongly Agree (5)

☐

I see a woman who knows her core values and their impact on her life.

☐

I see a woman who knows her strengths and areas of growth.

☐

I see a woman who understands the effect of white privilege and racism on her life.

☐

I see a woman who understands the effect of male privilege and sexism on her life.

☐

I see a woman who knows her purpose in life.

☐

I see a woman who knows how to manage her emotions effectively.

20/20 VISION

I AM

_____
_____
_____

I AM

_____
_____
_____

I AM

_____
_____
_____
_____
_____
_____
_____

20/20 VISION

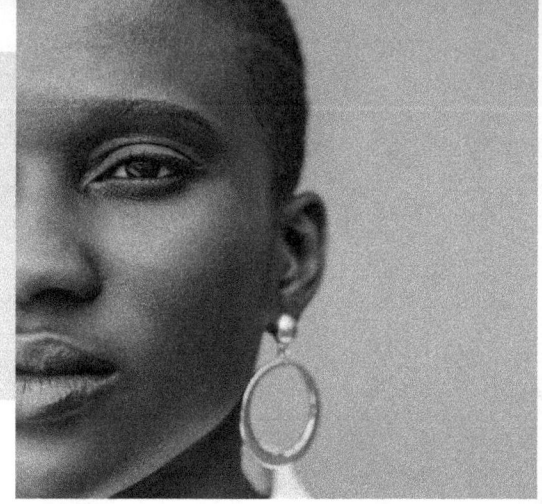

I AM

_____
_____
_____

I AM

_____
_____
_____

I AM

_____
_____
_____
_____
_____
_____

20/20 VISION

I LOVE

_____
_____
_____

I LOVE

_____
_____
_____

I LOVE

_____
_____
_____
_____
_____
_____
_____

20/20 VISION

I LOVE

_____
_____
_____

I LOVE

_____
_____
_____

I LOVE

_____
_____
_____
_____
_____
_____
_____

20/20 VISION

I DISLIKE

_____

_____

_____

I DISLIKE

_____

_____

_____

I DISLIKE

_____

_____

_____

_____

_____

_____

_____

20/20 VISION

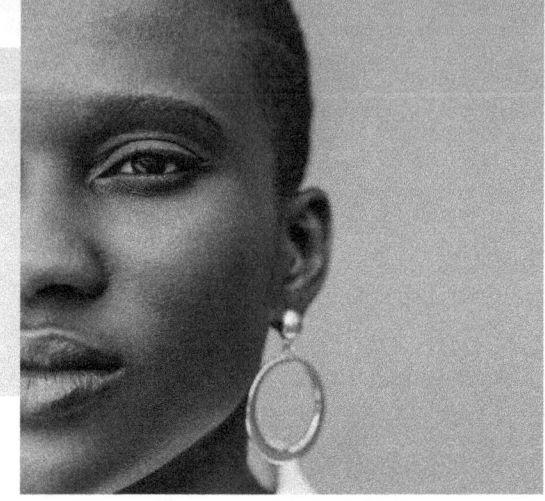

I DISLIKE

_____
_____
_____

I DISLIKE

_____
_____
_____

I DISLIKE

_____
_____
_____
_____
_____
_____
_____

20/20 VISION

I WANT TO STOP

_____
_____
_____

I WANT TO STOP

_____
_____
_____

I WANT TO STOP

_____
_____
_____
_____
_____
_____
_____

20/20 VISION

I WANT TO STOP

_____
_____
_____

I WANT TO STOP

_____
_____
_____

I WANT TO STOP

_____
_____
_____
_____
_____
_____

20/20 VISION

I WANT TO CONTINUE

_____
_____
_____

I WANT TO CONTINUE

_____
_____
_____

I WANT TO CONTINUE

_____
_____
_____
_____
_____
_____
_____

20/20 VISION

 I WANT TO CONTINUE

_____

_____

_____

I WANT TO CONTINUE

_____

_____

_____

I WANT TO CONTINUE

_____

_____

_____

_____

_____

_____

_____

20/20 VISION

I WANT TO BEGIN

_____
_____
_____

I WANT TO BEGIN

_____
_____
_____

I WANT TO BEGIN

_____
_____
_____
_____
_____
_____
_____

20/20 VISION

I WANT TO BEGIN

_____

_____

_____

I WANT TO BEGIN

_____

_____

_____

I WANT TO BEGIN

_____

_____

_____

_____

_____

_____

_____

APTITUDES, INTERESTS, & STRENGTHS

At Work

APTITUDES:
A natural ability or talent

INTERESTS:
Something or someone that sparks attention

STRENGTHS:
Skills, knowledge, talents, and proficiencies that are learned

APTITUDES, INTERESTS, & STRENGTHS

At Work

APTITUDES:
A natural ability or talent

INTERESTS:
Something or someone that sparks attention

STRENGTHS:
Skills, knowledge, talents, and proficiencies that are learned

APTITUDES, INTERESTS, & STRENGTHS

At Work

APTITUDES:
A natural ability or talent

INTERESTS:
Something or someone that sparks attention

STRENGTHS:
Skills, knowledge, talents, and proficiencies that are learned

APTITUDES, INTERESTS, & STRENGTHS

At School

APTITUDES:
A natural ability or talent

INTERESTS:
Something or someone that sparks attention

STRENGTHS:
Skills, knowledge, talents, and proficiencies that are learned

APTITUDES, INTERESTS, & STRENGTHS

At School

APTITUDES:
A natural ability or talent

INTERESTS:
Something or someone that sparks attention

STRENGTHS:
Skills, knowledge, talents, and proficiencies that are learned

APTITUDES, INTERESTS, & STRENGTHS

At School

APTITUDES:
A natural ability or talent

INTERESTS:
Something or someone that sparks attention

STRENGTHS:
Skills, knowledge, talents, and proficiencies that are learned

MY COMMUNITIES

Family, friends, social networks, professional
associations, athletic leagues, etc.

Communities where I feel comfortable and accepted

Communities where I feel less comfortable and/or unaccepted

_____

_____

_____

_____

Communities I would like to join or learn more about

MY COMMUNITIES

Family, friends, social networks, professional
associations, athletic leagues, etc.

Communities where I feel comfortable and accepted

Communities where I feel less comfortable and/or unaccepted

_____

_____

_____

_____

Communities I would like to join or learn more about

MY COMMUNITIES

Family, friends, social networks, professional associations, athletic leagues, etc.

Communities where I feel comfortable and accepted

Communities where I feel less comfortable and/or unaccepted

_____

_____

_____

_____

Communities I would like to join or learn more about

MY ALLIES

Allies are like air, water, and food—essential for survival.

HOME

WORK AND/OR
SCHOOL

COMMUNITY
(People and/or
Organizations)

MY ALLIES

Allies are like air, water, and food—essential for survival.

HOME

WORK AND/OR
SCHOOL

COMMUNITY
(People and/or
Organizations)

MY ALLIES

Allies are like air, water, and food—essential for survival.

HOME

WORK AND/OR SCHOOL

COMMUNITY (People and/or Organizations)

A TIME WHEN MY UNIQUENESS WAS NOT ACCEPTED, VALUED, AND/OR SUPPORTED

A TIME WHEN MY UNIQUENESS WAS NOT ACCEPTED, VALUED, AND/OR SUPPORTED

WHAT I NEED TO FEEL ACCEPTED, VALUED, AND SUPPORTED

HOME

WORK AND/OR SCHOOL

COMMUNITY
(People and/or Organizations)

WHAT I NEED TO FEEL ACCEPTED, VALUED, AND SUPPORTED

HOME

WORK AND/OR
SCHOOL

COMMUNITY
(People and/or
Organizations)

WHAT I NEED TO FEEL ACCEPTED, VALUED, AND SUPPORTED

HOME

WORK AND/OR SCHOOL

COMMUNITY (People and/or Organizations)

A TIME WHEN MY UNIQUENESS WAS ACCEPTED, VALUED, AND/OR SUPPORTED

A TIME WHEN MY UNIQUENESS WAS ACCEPTED, VALUED, AND/OR SUPPORTED

_____

_____

_____

_____

_____

_____

_____

_____

_____

_____

_____

_____

_____

_____

_____

_____

_____

_____

_____

_____

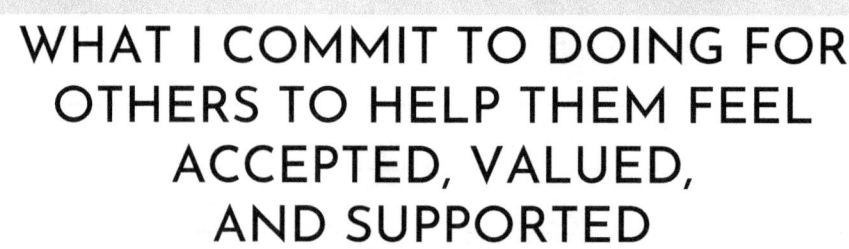

WHAT I COMMIT TO DOING FOR OTHERS TO HELP THEM FEEL ACCEPTED, VALUED, AND SUPPORTED

HOME

WORK AND/OR SCHOOL

COMMUNITY
(People and/or Organizations)

WHAT I COMMIT TO DOING FOR OTHERS TO HELP THEM FEEL ACCEPTED, VALUED, AND SUPPORTED

HOME

WORK AND/OR SCHOOL

COMMUNITY (People and/or Organizations)

WHAT DOES TRUST ...

LOOK LIKE?

1.

2.

3.

4.

SOUND LIKE?

_____
_____
_____
_____

FEEL LIKE?

_____
_____
_____

WHAT DOES TRUST ...

LOOK LIKE?

1.

2.

3.

4.

SOUND LIKE?

_____

_____

_____

_____

FEEL LIKE?

_____

_____

_____

HOW I CAN BUILD AND/OR REINFORCE TRUST IN MY COMMUNITIES

HOW I CAN BUILD AND/OR REINFORCE TRUST IN MY COMMUNITIES

TAKING CARE OF THE WHOLE ME IS SELF-CARE

"The more we practice deliberately caring for our well-being, the more resilient we become, which ultimately helps strengthen our ability to cope with and manage whatever comes our way in life."

SELF-CARE IS NOT A SIGN OF WEAKNESS, SELFISHNESS OR

the same for everyone.

SELF-CARE IS NECESSARY, INTENTIONAL, EVER-CHANGING, AND AN EXAMPLE OF

Self-love and compassion

Source: Suleman, K. (2019) Mental Health Match

283

FORMS OF SELF-CARE

EMOTIONAL

MENTAL

PHYSICAL

PRACTICAL

PROFESSIONAL

RELATIONAL

SPIRITUAL

MY SELF-CARE CHECKUP

☐ **Emotional wellbeing:** I engage in activities that help me explore, understand, and manage my emotions.

☐ **Mental wellbeing:** I engage in activities that help me calm my mind and reduce stress.

☐ **Physical wellbeing:** I engage in activities that help me maintain a healthy body.

☐ **Practical wellbeing:** I engage in activities that help me meet my core needs.

☐ **Professional wellbeing:** I engage in activities that help me be engaged, fulfilled, qualified, and safe.

☐ **Relational wellbeing:** I engage in activities that help me connect with those I care about and who cares about me.

☐ **Spiritual wellbeing:** I engage in activities (religious or non-religious) that help me nurture my soul and have a higher purpose than self.

MY SELF-CARE CHECKUP

Low (L)
Average (A)
High (H)
Maximum (M)

☐ **Emotional wellbeing:** I engage in activities that help me explore, understand, and manage my emotions.

☐ **Mental wellbeing:** I engage in activities that help me calm my mind and reduce stress.

☐ **Physical wellbeing:** I engage in activities that help me maintain a healthy body.

☐ **Practical wellbeing:** I engage in activities that help me meet my core needs.

☐ **Professional wellbeing:** I engage in activities that help me be engaged, fulfilled, qualified, and safe.

☐ **Relational wellbeing:** I engage in activities that help me connect with those I care about and who cares about me.

☐ **Spiritual wellbeing:** I engage in activities (religious or non-religious) that help me nurture my soul and have a higher purpose than self.

MY SELF-CARE CHECKUP

Low (L)
Average (A)
High (H)
Maximum (M)

☐ **Emotional wellbeing:** I engage in activities that help me explore, understand, and manage my emotions.

☐ **Mental wellbeing:** I engage in activities that help me calm my mind and reduce stress.

☐ **Physical wellbeing:** I engage in activities that help me maintain a healthy body.

just breathe

☐ **Practical wellbeing:** I engage in activities that help me meet my core needs.

☐ **Professional wellbeing:** I engage in activities that help me be engaged, fulfilled, qualified, and safe.

☐ **Relational wellbeing:** I engage in activities that help me connect with those I care about and who cares about me.

LEVEL UP

☐ **Spiritual wellbeing:** I engage in activities (religious or non-religious) that help me nurture my soul and have a higher purpose than self.

MY SELF-CARE CHECKUP

Low (L)
Average (A)
High (H)
Maximum (M)

☐ I get enough sleep, rest, and relaxation to recharge my mind and body.

☐ I engage in regular physical activities that aid in movement, endurance, and strength.

GOAL Getter

☐ I eat healthy, balanced meals everyday--plenty of fruits, vegetables, and water.

☐ I maintain a work-life balance.

☐ I increase my knowledge and skills, and cultivate my talents.

☐ I foster positive, affirming relationships with family, friends, and colleagues.

GAME ON

☐ I live a life of purpose and meaning--engaging in passion projects and works.

MY SELF-CARE CHECKUP

Low (L)
Average (A)
High (H)
Maximum (M)

☐ I get enough sleep, rest, and relaxation to recharge my mind and body.

☐ I engage in regular physical activities that aid in movement, endurance, and strength.

GOAL
Getter

☐ I eat healthy, balanced meals everyday--plenty of fruits, vegetables, and water.

☐ I maintain a work-life balance.

☐ I increase my knowledge and skills, and cultivate my talents.

☐ I foster positive, affirming relationships with family, friends, and colleagues.

GAME ON

☐ I live a life of purpose and meaning--engaging in passion projects and works.

MY SELF-CARE CHECKUP

Low (L)
Average (A)
High (H)
Maximum (M)

- [ ] I get enough sleep, rest, and relaxation to recharge my mind and body.

- [ ] I engage in regular physical activities that aid in movement, endurance, and strength.

GOAL Getter

- [ ] I eat healthy, balanced meals everyday--plenty of fruits, vegetables, and water.

- [ ] I maintain a work-life balance.

- [ ] I increase my knowledge and skills, and cultivate my talents.

- [ ] I foster positive, affirming relationships with family, friends, and colleagues.

GAME ON

- [ ] I live a life of purpose and meaning--engaging in passion projects and works.

A WEEK OF SELF-CARE

New Self-Care Activities

Goal:

Steps I will take to achieve my goal:

A WEEK OF SELF-CARE

New Self-Care Activities

Goal:

Steps I will take to achieve my goal:

A WEEK OF SELF-CARE

New Self-Care Activities

Goal:

Steps I will take to achieve my goal:

WEEKLY PLANNER

MONDAY

TUESDAY

WEDNESDAY

THURSDAY

FRIDAY

NOTES

_____

_____

_____

_____

_____

_____

_____

_____

294

WEEKLY PLANNER

MONDAY

TUESDAY

WEDNESDAY

THURSDAY

FRIDAY

NOTES

_____

_____

_____

_____

_____

_____

_____

WEEKLY PLANNER

MONDAY

TUESDAY

WEDNESDAY

THURSDAY

FRIDAY

NOTES

_____

_____

_____

_____

_____

_____

_____

_____

MY WEEK OF SELF-CARE ACTIVITIES

MONDAY

TUESDAY

WEDNESDAY

THURSDAY

FRIDAY

WEEKEND

MY WEEK OF SELF-CARE ACTIVITIES

MONDAY

TUESDAY

WEDNESDAY

THURSDAY

FRIDAY

WEEKEND

MY WEEK OF
SELF-CARE ACTIVITIES

MONDAY

TUESDAY

WEDNESDAY

THURSDAY

FRIDAY

WEEKEND

MY WEEK OF SELF-CARE

REFLECTION

_____
_____
_____
_____
_____
_____
_____
_____
_____
_____
_____
_____
_____
_____
_____
_____
_____
_____
_____
_____
_____

MY WEEK OF SELF-CARE

REFLECTION

_____
_____
_____
_____
_____
_____
_____
_____
_____
_____
_____
_____
_____
_____
_____
_____
_____

MY WEEK OF SELF-CARE

REFLECTION

_____
_____
_____
_____
_____
_____
_____
_____
_____
_____
_____
_____
_____
_____
_____
_____
_____
_____
_____
_____
_____
_____
_____

A Month of Joy

Activities for my self-love month of joy

DATE   ACTIVITY

_____

_____

_____

_____

_____

_____

_____

_____

A Month of Joy

Activities for my self-love month of joy

DATE   ACTIVITY

_____
_____
_____
_____
_____
_____
_____
_____
_____
_____
_____

A Month
of Joy

Activities for my self-love month of joy

DATE   ACTIVITY

_____

_____

_____

_____

_____

_____

_____

_____

MY MONTH OF JOY

REFLECTION

_____
_____
_____
_____
_____
_____
_____
_____
_____
_____
_____
_____

MY MONTH OF JOY

REFLECTION

_____

_____

_____

_____

_____

_____

_____

_____

_____

_____

MY MONTH OF JOY

REFLECTION

_____
_____
_____
_____
_____
_____
_____
_____
_____
_____
_____

N. D. Jones, Ed.D. is a USA Today bestselling author who lives in Maryland with her husband and two young adult children. In her desire to see more novels with positive, sexy, and three-dimensional African American characters as soul mates, friends, and lovers, she took on that challenge herself. Along with the fantasy romance series Forever Yours, and a contemporary romance trilogy, The Styles of Love, she has authored three paranormal romance series: Winged Warriors, Death and Destiny, and Dragon Shifter Romance, and two fantasy series: Feline Nation and Fairy Tale Fatale.

N. D. is also the founder of Kuumba Publishing, an art, audiobook, eBook, and paperback company that is a forum for creativity, with a special commitment to promoting and encouraging creative works from authors and artists of African descent.

BOOKS BY N.D. JONES

Fantasy in Black (Coloring Book Series)
Spread Your Wings and Fly: Black Women Fairies Coloring Book (Book 1)
Be UnBound: Black Male Angels Coloring Book (Book 2)

Winged Warriors Trilogy (Paranormal Romance)
Fire, Fury, Faith (Book 1)
Heat, Hunt, Hope (Book 2)
Lies, Lust, Love (Book 3)

Death and Destiny Trilogy (Paranormal Romance)
Of Fear and Faith (Book 1)
Of Beasts and Bonds (Book 2)
Of Deception and Divinity (Book 3)

Forever Yours Series (Afrofuturism)
Bound Souls (Book 1)
Fated Path (Book 2)

Dragon Shifter Romance (Standalone Novels)
Stones of Dracontias: The Bloodstone Dragon
Dragon Lore and Love: Isis and Osiris

The Styles of Love Trilogy (Contemporary Romance)
The Perks of Higher Ed (Book 1)
The Wish of Xmas Present (Book 2)
The Gift of Second Chances (Book 3)

BOOKS BY N.D. JONES

Fairy Tale Fatale Series (Urban Fantasy)
Crimson Hunter: A Red Riding Hood Reimagining
Bearly Gold: Goldilocks and the Three Bears Reimagining

Feline Nation Duology (Urban Fantasy)
A Queen's Pride (Book 1)
Mafdet's Claws (Book 2)

REFERENCES

6 Different Types of Abuse. (2017, March 23). Retrieved August 28, 2020, from https://reachma.org/6-different-types-abuse/

7 Types Of Self-Care & Why You Need Them. (2019, December 05). Retrieved August 28, 2020, from https://www.healthcoachinstitute.com/motivational/7-types-of-self-care/

Ackerman, C. E. (2020, June 09). What is Resilience and Why is It Important to Bounce Back? Retrieved August 28, 2020, from https://positivepsychology.com/what-is-resilience/

Bond-Theriault, C. (2020, June 26). 14 Black LGBTQ Folks on How They're Taking Care of Themselves Right Now. Retrieved August 28, 2020, from https://www.self.com/story/black-lgbtq-self-care-tips

Boyd, K. (2020, February 4). 50 Inspiring Quotes from Famous Black Women to Celebrate Black History Month. Retrieved September 04, 2020, from https://cafemom.com/entertainment/210615-50-quotes-from-black-women

Building Your Resilience. (2012). Retrieved August 28, 2020, from https://www.apa.org/topics/resilience

Centers for Disease Control and Prevention. (2019, November 20). Leading Causes of Death-Non-Hispanic black Females - United States, 2017. Retrieved September 04, 2020, from https://www.cdc.gov/women/lcod/2017/nonhispanic-black/index.htm

REFERENCES

Cohen, H. (2020, July 30). What is
Resilience? Retrieved August 28, 2020, from
https://psychcentral.com/lib/what-is-resilience/

Deanna. (2018, September 28).
Professional Self Care Mindset Tools for the Stressed Out Career Girl.
Retrieved August 28, 2020, from https://www.morningcoffeewithdee.com/professional-self-care/

DeShay, A. (2020, July 12). Black Women Statistics. Retrieved September 04, 2020,
from
https://blackdemographics.com/population/black-women-statistics/

Health Coach Institute. (2019,
December 02). 60 Healthy Self-Care Ideas To Feel Better Than Ever. Retrieved
August 28, 2020, from https://www.healthcoachinstitute.com/motivational/60-healthy-self-care-ideas-to-feel-better-than-ever/

Jeffrey, S. (2020, June 26). Core
Values List: Over 200 Personal Values to Live By Today. Retrieved August 28, 2020,
from https://scottjeffrey.com/core-values-list/

Luna, A. (2021, August 3). How to Identify Your Emotional Triggers (Before it's Too
Late) LonerWolf. Retrieved August 30, 2021, from
https://lonerwolf.com/emotional-triggers/

REFERENCES

Mental Health America. (2020). Black and African American Communities and Mental Health. Retrieved September 04, 2020, from https://www.mhanational.org/issues/black-and-african-american-communities-and-mental-health

Merriam Webster. (n.d.).
Resilience. Retrieved August 29, 2020, from https://www.merriam-webster.com/dictionary/resilience

Pietrangelo, A. (2001, April 17).
64 Signs of Mental and Emotional Abuse: How to Identify It, What to Do. Retrieved August 28, 2020, from https://www.healthline.com/health/signs-of-mental-abuse

Planned Parenthood. (2020). Six
Types of Self Care. Retrieved August 28, 2020, from https://secure.everyaction.com/p/Pg5bqblugE6-NGId09RIcQ2

Resilience. (2020). Retrieved
August 28, 2020, from https://www.dictionary.com/browse/resilience

Shine. (2018, February 26). 13 Powerful Quotes From Black Women About Self-Love. Retrieved September 04, 2020, from https://advice.shinetext.com/articles/quotes-from-powerful-black-women-all-about-self-love/

REFERENCES

Suleman, K. (2019, November 20).
"What Does "Self-Care" Actually Mean and Why Am I Supposed to be
Doing it on Sundays?" Retrieved August 28, 2020, from
https://ajanatherapy.com/what-does-self-care-actually-mean-and-why-am-i-supposed-
to-be-doing-it-on-sundays/

Tartakovsky, M. (2019, March 31).
The 7 Vital Types Of Self-Care. Retrieved August 28, 2020, from
https://blogs.psychcentral.com/weightless/2011/05/the-7-vital-types-of-self-care/

Universal Emotions: What are
Emotions? (2020, January 30). Retrieved August 28, 2020, from
https://www.paulekman.com/universal-emotions/

U.S. Department of Health and Human Services Office of Minority Health. (2019,
September 25). Mental and Behavioral Health - African Americans. Retrieved
September 04, 2020, from https://minorityhealth.hhs.gov/omh/browse.aspx?lvl=4

Wayne State University-Division of
Student Affairs. (n.d.). Self-Care. Retrieved August 28, 2020, from
https://www.wright.edu/student-affairs/health-and-wellness/counseling-and-
wellness/workshops-and-self-help/self-care

N. D. JONES

CPSIA information can be obtained
at www.ICGtesting.com
Printed in the USA
BVHW010912180322
631762BV00016B/586